LIVING
IN
THE USA

SIXTH EDITION

Praise for *Living in the U.S.A.*

"Jef Davis' insight and honesty help the reader make sense of the complicated and conflicting realities of the U.S.A. today. This sixth edition of *Living in the U.S.A.* provides analysis of current issues (ethnic co-cultures, diverse family structures, obesity, mobil phone plans, educational system choices), exposes long-held myths about the U.S., and provides a fresh perspective on the familiar (size, people). While written for the newcomer, I believe any American reader will learn much about his or her own culture."
—Dianne Hofner Saphiere, creator, Cultural Detective,
www.culturaldetective.com, and principal, Nipporica

"In this sixth edition of *Living in the U.S.A.* Jef Davis provides a first-rate update of the practical information and the insights into contemporary U.S. culture, adding a frank and accessible discussion of the complexities of life in twenty-first-century U.S.A. A must read for any sojourner to the U.S."
—Ann Kuhlman, director, office of International Students and Scholars,
Yale University

"*Living in the U.S.A.* succeeds in illustrating the complexities of American life without becoming overwhelming. Jef Davis has provided visitors to the U.S. with an indispensable and amazingly thorough tool for navigating the complexities of American society."
—Katherine S. Hammett, director, International Student Services,
Xavier University

"This sixth edition of *Living in the U.S.A.* integrates the best from the thiry-year-old classic with a remarkably objective picture of the socio-political context of present-day America. It can be argued that the country today offers its newcomers as potentially confusing and adverse a welcome as ever; Jef Davis has done an impressive job of explaining the dynamics that make this so and of offering pathways to a rich and deeply textured understanding of the U.S."
—Barbara F. Schaetti, Ph.D., principal, consultant, transition dynamics
and senior associate, The Crestone Institute

LIVING
IN
THE USA

SIXTH EDITION

ALISON R. LANIER ☆ REVISED BY JEF C. DAVIS

INTERCULTURAL PRESS
A Nicholas Brealey Publishing Company

YARMOUTH, ME · BOSTON · LONDON

Published by Intercultural Press, a Nicholas Brealey Publishing Company, in 2005

Intercultural Press, Inc.,
a Nicholas Brealey Publishing Company
PO Box 700
Yarmouth, Maine 04096 USA
Tel: 207-846-5168
Fax: 207-846-5181
www.interculturalpress.com

Nicholas Brealey Publishing
3-5 Spafield Street, Clerkenwell
London, EC1R 4QB, UK

Tel: +44-(0)-207-239-0360
Fax: +44-(0)-207-239-0370
www.nbrealey-books.com

Printed in the United States of America

09   08   07   06   05   1 ·2   3   4   5

ISBN 1-931930-19-8

Library of Congress Cataloging-in-Publication Data

Lanier, Alison Raymond.
    Living in the U.S.A. / Alison R. Lanier.—6th ed. / rev. by Jef C. Davis.
        p. cm.
    Includes bibliographical references and index.
    ISBN 1-931930-19-8
    1. United States—Social life and customs—1971– 2. United States—
Guidebooks. I. Davis, Jef C., 1964– II. Title.
    E169.O2L26 2005
    973.92—dc22
                    2004024867

For Alonzo and Lydia,

who give meaning to everything we do,

and for Natacha,

who inspires me.

Table of Contents

Acknowledgments

I would like to thank Judy Carl-Hendrick of Intercultural Press for her encouragement, her confidence in me, and her guidance about what to include in this revision. Thanks are due to my wife Natacha and to her parents, all three of them immigrants to the United States, for their observations about my country and for giving me the time away from child rearing to write. I am also grateful to my parents for helping me along the way.

I would also like to acknowledge the thousands of foreign students and faculty I have worked with over the last twenty years, as well as their families, for their perceptions of living in the United States, and to thank N. Kirk Robey, who gave me my first opportunity to work with foreign students. While the views presented here have been influenced by the many world citizens I have known, omissions and oversights are mine alone.

Original Preface

This book stems from conversations with countless people from all over the world. I am grateful for their thoughtful contributions to it.

The book was first published in 1973 by Charles Scribner's Sons. Since then it has been revised, updated, and republished in many paperback editions. It has also been published in nine other countries and seven languages.

The book grew out of the experiences of my own firm, Overseas Briefing Associates, which worked for many years with U.S. and foreign personnel, helping them adjust to unfamiliar countries and conditions.

I hope this guide to American life will ease your path and help you to understand the vast land and varied people that make up these United States.

Alison R. Lanier

Introduction

Writing an introductory guide to one's own country is an opportunity for cultural and personal self-reflection. In this sixth edition of *Living in the U.S.A.*, I have tried to retain the flavor, perceptions, and insights of the earlier editions, while infusing it with updated factual information and some of my own observations of my country. I hope that fans of the late Alison Lanier's early editions, as well as Bill Gay's more recent one, will find their favorite sections and points of view faithfully rendered, but changing times also require changing perspectives. As Bill observed in the forward to the fifth edition, things change fast in this country, and indeed there is much that is new in this edition.

Along with updated demographic, legal, and procedural information, I have attempted to place the United States into its current context, that of the early twenty-first century. When the last edition was published, the Soviet Union had been dissolved for just four years, William Jefferson Clinton was still in his first term as president, the U.S. economy was booming, and the World Trade Center stood as a beacon of financial might. As I finish this edition, there is a hotly contested presidential race, U.S. military forces are attempting to manage the transition to Iraqi self-rule, and the effects of September 11, 2001, continue to reverberate throughout our political and social lives. The impact of the wars in Afghanistan and especially in Iraq will no doubt shape how Americans see themselves, and how the world sees us, for some time to come. Clearly, we are still coming to terms with the obligations and limitations of our status as the world's sole remaining military superpower.

Living in the U.S.A. occupies an unusual place among books intended to familiarize people from other countries with the United States. It is not merely a cultural exploration designed to help newcomers understand Americans better, although such information is included throughout the book, in particular in Chapters 2 and 3.* Neither is *Living in the U.S.A.* a relocation guide packed with local resources specific to a particular metropolitan area. Such a booklet may be available from the Chamber of Commerce of your new city, or from the international office of a nearby university.

For its part, *Living in the U.S.A.* lies somewhere in between, more practical than a cultural analysis and more general than a city relocation guide. It can help you understand how cultural traits will likely affect your daily interactions with Americans, and it will provide you with the terminology and the range of options you have, whether you are shopping for housing or for countless other goods and services. It is intended as a practical guide, to point you toward resources and to help you ask the right questions, with a better understanding of the results you might find.

Readers familiar with earlier editions of this book will notice, along with new and updated sections, significant reorganization. Part I, "American Intangibles," is devoted to demographic and geographic features of the country and its people. Chapter 2, for example, brings together observations about our dominant culture to produce (I hope) a coherent and expanded chapter about cultural norms. Although cultural diversity is much too large for a single chapter (or even a single book), Chapter 3 explores this topic in more detail and includes additional four cocultural groups: Native Americans, retired people, Americans with disabilities, and gay, lesbian, bisexual, and transgendered Americans.

Part II, "American Institutions," chronicles the ways that we as Americans organize our lives. Chapter 4, "American Social Life," combines customs, manners, friendships, and dating. Chapter 7, "American Family Life," is an updated look at the many possible configurations of the American family, including new sections on single-parent and blended families, gay and lesbian families, and dual-career couples. Chapter 8, "American Business Life," covers a variety of workplace issues, from labor unions to life in the office.

Part III addresses the practical matters of being admitted to the United States and getting settled here. New sections on immigration and customs describe the new procedures and requirements for visiting the United

---

*For an excellent book devoted to explaining American culture, see Gary Althen's *American Ways* or Milton Bennet's and Edward Stewart's *American Cultural Patterns*. For a detailed explanation of how to work effectively with Americans, see Craig Storti's *Americans at Work*.

States. Chapter 10, "Money and Banking," has been updated as well. Chapter 13 includes two new sections: obesity and health food. "Staying in Touch with People," Chapter 14, includes new sections on choosing cell phone plans and Internet service providers.

Part IV, "For Those Who Stay Longer," provides in-depth information on setting up a new life here in the United States. Chapter 16, "Housing," now includes the basics of buying a home as well as of renting one, and Chapter 19, "Educating Your Children," has been enlarged to help newcomers better understand the available choices our educational system provides.

In short, the sixth edition of *Living in the U.S.A.* is an attempt to anticipate what you as a newcomer will need and want to know. Also new in this edition are websites for the resources listed throughout the book, and other chapters have been significantly updated as well.

In the last chapter, an afterword, I have laid out some of the most pressing issues that we as a nation must continue to face in the coming decades, as a country and as people. If you, the reader, should decide to make the United States your home, these will become your issues as well.

The term *American* is sometimes contested when used to refer exclusively to inhabitants of the United States of America, conflicting as it does with a sense of Pan-American identity often found in South America, Central America, Mexico, and Canada. Unfortunately, the English language lacks a graceful alternative such as the Spanish *estadouenses* or the French *etats-unisiens*. *American* remains the term that most of us use to describe ourselves, and for this book I have chosen not to break with that tradition.

Any discussion that deals with a group of people may tend to stereotype, and this book is no exception. It may be helpful to remember, however, the differences between a stereotype and a generalization.

A generalization is really a statistical statement about a population. Take, for example, the statement, "Americans tend to be uninformed about other countries." As a generalization, this means merely that compared with the inhabitants of other countries with similar economic and educational advantages, Americans *as a group* generally score lower on a test of world knowledge than the inhabitants of many other countries. Knowing this, however, does little to help you to accurately predict whether any particular American will have substantial knowledge of the larger world. She or he may very well have a university degree in Latin American studies or in East Asian history!

As you can see, this generalization could also be a stereotype. When you meet an American, you might *assume* that person is ignorant about your country, and treat him or her accordingly. You may well be surprised to learn, however, that this particular American has traveled to your homeland, read about it in the newspaper, or even studied your language. Also, when we stereotype, we tend to ignore statements that challenge our notions and to emphasize those that reinforce them.

Americans have a tendency to resist being categorized more than most other people. As self-made individualists, we strongly prefer to attribute our identities to our own choices and personal beliefs. We like to believe that we are too diverse a country to make generalizations about; of course, that doesn't stop us from being quick to generalize about (or even stereotype) other nationalities or ethnic groups. Nevertheless, because I have chosen to retain a conversational tone in this book, I refer to Americans as "we," even when discussing generalizations that do not necessarily represent my own point of view.

Visitors and newcomers to the United States today will find a people better informed about the world than in previous times, but also a people caught up in a tension between cultural and political isolationism, on the one hand, and global involvement on the other. Foreigners, especially those from the Middle Eastern and other largely Muslim countries, should be prepared for a heightened level of suspicion on the part of some Americans. Despite this, and despite new bureaucratic barriers to coming to the U.S., you will find that many Americans are still eager to get to know foreigners, and if you make the effort to get to know us, you will soon find yourself among friends.

Part I

American Intangibles

1

First Impressions

t is probably fair to say that almost anyone in the world knows more about the United States than the average American knows about any other person's country. News channels like CNN broadcast by satellite twenty-four hours a day around the world. American musical forms are still the most popular in many countries, especially among young people. Movies made in Hollywood are available in theaters and on DVD in almost every country, and U.S. entertainment television programs are among the favorites of people from Baku to Bamako. In fact, you may very well feel saturated with — even bombarded by — images of the United States. But while movies and television programs depict distinct aspects of American life, they cannot begin to prepare you for the complexity of real life here. Similarly, books you might have read, even this one, can give only a limited picture of what life will be like. No matter how prepared you think you are for moving to a new country, you can easily be overwhelmed by your first impressions.

Relocation to the United States is frequently a difficult transition, even though a chance to live in a new culture is an exciting prospect for most people. Newcomers have many questions: Where will we live? Where can we find household help? How difficult is it to buy a car? What kinds of taxes must be paid and when? What customs and courtesies are different from those in our country? What medical services are available? The list seems endless.

It is easier and (in relative terms) cheaper than ever to move from one corner of the globe to another by jet. International trade has led to increasing interaction among nations, and with this comes the transfer of diplomats, businesspeople, executives, professors, and students — often accompanied by spouses and families.

Pace

One of the first things many people comment on upon arriving in the United States is the pace of life here. Because they arrive by jet, the first impression visitors usually have of the United States is in one of the major cities, where the pace of life is fast. People are in a rush to get where they are going, waiting impatiently to be served a meal, restlessly seeking attention in a store, bumping into other people as they walk quickly along the street. Bus and taxi drivers may not seem friendly, waiters may hurry you, and department store salespeople may not spend much time with you. You may not see many smiles, it may be difficult to have a conversation with strangers, and you may get lost in the crowds. All this can be frightening and confusing unless you are accustomed to city life in your own country. Don't take such behavior personally; this is life in the city. The pace is gentler outside the big metropolises, as it is in other countries.

Americans who live in cities assume that everyone is in a hurry and is self-sufficient, and that people know where they are going and how to get there, just as city people do in Tokyo or Paris, Cairo or São Paulo. If you need assistance or want to ask a question, people who work in hotels, department stores, restaurants, shops, and many other places will usually help you if you ask them in a friendly manner. Friendliness will almost always be returned. *But you must let people know that you need help;* otherwise, they may not notice you because most Americans use a direct style of communication, as we shall see in Chapter 2. While you might see a lost person in need of help, an American might see only a self-sufficient person studying a map. As in any large city, a few people may not respond in a helpful manner. If this happens, don't be discouraged; just ask someone else. Most Americans enjoy helping a stranger.

People

Unless you have spent time in some of the world's cosmopolitan centers, the incredible diversity of people in the U.S. is sure to stand out. People of African, Asian, European, and American ancestry all bustle about the city. You will likely hear Spanish, Amharic, Cantonese, Mandarin, and dialects of English you've never heard before — all in the space of a few blocks in New York or San Francisco.

Of the more than 290 million people who call the United States home, most have their origins in other parts of the world. The names you see over shop doors tell you so, as do the varied types of faces you pass on the streets. A roll call of schoolchildren will include such names as Adams, Ali, Bykowski, Capparella, Fujita, Gonzales, Mukerji, Nusseibeh, and Wong. Mostly, people from these diverse backgrounds have not been blended in the so-called American "melting pot." In fact, the idea that the United States is a melting pot is largely a myth. Instead, many ethnic groups retain at least some of their own customs and social traditions (for more about ethnic and cultural diversity in the United States, see Chapter 3). They merge into the American mainstream only in certain aspects of life — in school, sports, and business, to name a few — but keep to many of their own cultural patterns socially and in their homes. Each successive generation becomes a little more removed from its ancestral homeland.

For many Christians of European ancestry, intermarriage eventually blends nationalities together. It is quite common to hear that someone is "mostly Irish, with a lot of French and a little Dutch on my mother's side" or "Heinz 57 — a little bit of everything." Unfortunately, racial, ethnic, and cultural differences continue to divide Americans, and the option of blending in is not equally available to everyone, nor is it always desired. Many people who are not of European descent resist the idea that they should "blend in," which can be perceived as giving up their own culture for one that reflects only European values. Many recent immigrants, however, are among the country's most patriotic citizens.

Many tensions now apparent in American life originate from the interaction of varied cultures. Nonetheless, you will be able to find your own familiar world here — be it in spices or fruits, churches or national groups, newspapers or music.

Another aspect of our people that immediately stands out to newcomers is our friendliness. Especially when you get away from the big cities, you will find it easy to engage us in conversation, you'll see us letting you go first in line, and you'll see us smiling — lots and lots of smiling. In fact, we smile so much, even at strangers, that many newcomers become nervous. They may fear that we are idiots, that we are planning to rob them, or that we are making amorous advances. The simple truth is, we simply tend to smile more often and more broadly at strangers than do people in many other cultures.

Size

The United States is big — really *big*. About half the size of the Russian Federation in area, the U.S. is bigger than China or Brazil and is nearly a third the size of all of Africa. At 9,631,418 square kilometers (according to the *CIA Factbook*), it is two and a half times the size of Western Europe. Unless you are from a very large country, it is probably difficult to imagine how vast the U.S. is. It is not an easy matter to experience, or "feel" the size of the United States, even when you know the actual number of miles from coast to coast. One way to think about it is to compare distances within the United States with other distances more familiar to you. For example, the distance from New York to Washington, D.C., is about the same as from London to Paris, or Nairobi to Mombassa, or Tokyo to Kyoto; New York to Los Angeles is farther than Lisbon to Cairo, or Moscow to Montreal, or New Delhi to Rome. It takes about the same length of time to fly from New York to Los Angeles as it does to fly from New York to London.

It is difficult for people who come from smaller countries to realize how important this matter of size is in the lives of Americans. Not only is the country vast, it also contains nearly 300 million people. These two factors affect every phase of life, not only creating a highly competitive domestic market for goods, which gives rise to constant advertising, but also causing an equally competitive political arena. Wide geographic differences make for profound differences in attitudes and values. A New Englander, for example, often has a quite different point of view than a Texan, and a Hawaiian may not understand the values of a Minnesotan. Marked differences in geography or weather and widely dispersed ethnic heritages naturally affect people's attitudes — but in the United States such differences occur within the same nation. An overseas visitor once remarked, "No wonder Americans talk so loud and move so fast. In a place that size you almost have to or you get lost in the shuffle."

It is not only our land that is big. Our roads, our cars, and our sport utility vehicles are big. Our dinner plates are big. Our Rocky Mountains are big. Our Great Plains are big, and our Great Lakes look more like seas than lakes. For many of us, our waistlines are big as well (see Chapter 13).

Another way to comprehend the vastness of the United States is to be aware of the time changes. There are four different time zones between the two coasts. When it is 12:00 noon Eastern Standard Time in New York, it is 11:00 A.M. Central Standard Time in Chicago, 10:00 A.M. Mountain Standard Time in Denver, and 9:00 A.M. Pacific Standard Time in San Francisco.

Canada, being wider from east to west, adds one more time zone: Atlantic Standard Time for New Brunswick, Prince Edward Island, Nova Scotia, Newfoundland, and Labrador. Alaska (the forty-ninth state of the United States, but not adjoining) extends even farther west than Canada and adds an additional two time zones, Alaska Standard Time and Nome Standard Time. Hawaii (the fiftieth state) is a group of islands in the Pacific Ocean, about 2,400 miles (4,000 kilometers) west of the U.S. mainland. Since it is directly south of Alaska, it uses Alaska Standard Time. The American continent is so wide that it encompasses *one-third* of all the world's time zones.

The world's date line is halfway around the world from zero meridian, that is, twelve hours away from Greenwich, on the 180th meridian. East of this imaginary line, the calendar is a day earlier than points west of it. People coming to the United States from Asia will therefore add a day to their lives — until they go home again, when they will lose a day.

Climate

Naturally, with such distances, the climate in the continental United States is also one of great extremes. From New England and New York through Chicago and much of the Midwest and Northwest, temperatures vary from subzero in winter to the high nineties or over (Fahrenheit) in summer.

The South and the Southwest have warmer weather, though even these sections have occasional frosts and periods of moderate cold. Generally, summers are likely to range from 70°F to 110°F (21°C to 43°C), and many areas can be quite humid. However, air conditioning is so widespread that you can expect most buildings — even many private homes and apartments — to be kept at relatively comfortable temperatures. Alaskan temperatures are, of course, extremely cold most of the year, while Hawaii enjoys a very moderate climate year-round. Temperatures there are normally in the seventies and eighties (Fahrenheit).

2

Dominant U.S. American Values

Because the United States is such a diverse country, it may at first seem impossible to describe a central common culture. In one sense, this is true: there are so many cultural groups here that there is no single set of cultural values that represents every group. In addition, there is also tremendous variation *within groups*, so that the opposite of any true statement might also be true, at least for some members of some groups. That being said, most experts will agree that there is a *dominant U.S. American culture*, a culture that is pervasive enough among people with influence that social, political, and business life will reflect that culture and its norms.

Because we are a diverse country with a strong emphasis on individualism, we are likely to notice things that make us different from one another. You will most likely soon be able to identify aspects of our culture that bind us together. It should come as no surprise that in the United States, the dominant culture is that shared by European Americans. And because European Americans have long run the institutions of government, education, and commerce, you will likely find that these institutions reflect European American values. In this chapter we will explore some of those dominant cultural traits.

There is no doubt that many of our customs and cultural traits will surprise you; the same thing happens to us when we visit another country. People living in various cultures handle many small daily activities differently. Some differences are minor, and one soon becomes accustomed to them. You may find the transitory quality of much of American life odd — the fact, for example, that one can rent art by the week or the entire furnishings for an apartment, from sofa and beds to the last spoon, on a few hours' notice. Supermarkets offer a wide variety of packaged foods that busy people can prepare quickly so that they can spend more time in recreational activities than in domestic chores. Large chain stores located in huge warehouses offer discount prices for goods sold in bulk packaging. "Packaged" living is part of today's American scene, part of its mobility and pace.

At the same time — perhaps even *because* of a sense of impermanence — houses are of great interest to Americans. We spend much time thinking and reading and talking about the design of houses, their decorations, how to improve them. Many weekend hours are passed in "do-it-yourself" projects around the house. People also love to look at each other's houses. Since we would thoroughly enjoy visiting and examining a house in another country, we assume that you will probably have the same desire. Don't be surprised, therefore, if when you visit someone you are shown the entire house from top to bottom, including bathrooms and closets. Don't make the mistake of declining the offer; the whole house may have been cleaned especially for you.

Because our people have come from so many nationalities, there is a far wider range of acceptable behavior than in countries where the inhabitants have grown up with a common heritage. As a result, you won't need to feel awkward or uncomfortable in following your own customs. Although Americans are noticeably informal, if you prefer somewhat greater formality, feel free to act in your own way. This will likely be acceptable to those around you. To a very large extent, you can "do your own thing" and be respected here.

However, it may help to have a little guidance in understanding some general cultural patterns in the United States. Cultural traits are much less obvious than everyday customs — and much more important to you in getting along with Americans. The subject is, of course, too broad and the ethnic differences too great to cover fully, but a few common patterns are worth mentioning.

Egalitarianism

If you come from a country where rank is clearly recognized and deferred to, you may miss the lack of protocol. For example, we rarely seat an honored guest in a particular position in the dining room, living room, or in a car. A few formalities do exist, however; you may observe that the honored guest will normally sit to the right of the host or hostess at a dinner party and will probably be shown through a door or into an elevator first. But other than honored, usually first-time guests, Americans expect to be treated equally in social situations.

Informality

American informality is well known. Many new arrivals interpret it as a lack of respect when they first encounter it, especially in the business world. The almost immediate use of first names, for example, may be a shock to those long accustomed to being status conscious, since the use of first names in some cultures signals a fair degree of intimacy.

Don't be surprised if Americans do not shake hands, especially in informal situations. They often just nod or smile instead. A casual "Hi" or "How are you doing?" or "Hello" often takes the place of a formal handshake but means the same thing. Nor will you find Americans circulating among fellow office workers or people at a party giving each one a personal farewell. Instead — again the different sense of timing and pace — they will just wave a cheery "good-bye" or say something informal to the whole group, such as "Well, see you tomorrow" or "So long, everybody." Then they will leave, again without handshakes.

You will see even high-level executives working at their desks in shirtsleeves, sometimes without ties. They may lean far back in their chairs in a casual manner while they talk on the telephone. This is not meant to be rude. Once we get out of the tense, hurried city streets, we are an informal people.

Our pace is often either totally hurried, intense, work-absorbed, and competitive (in play as well as work) or else totally at ease and informal, a relaxed manner described as "laid-back." We tend to swing between these extremes, and you need to understand this pendulum if you are to comprehend the United States and its people.

It has been said that while Americans are friendly, we don't necessarily make good friends. Researchers have shown that this statement is perfectly true, depending on your definition of *friend*.

To many Americans, a friend is just about anyone with whom we have friendly relations. This may include co-workers, classmates, friends of friends, and many other acquaintances. In fact, the term *acquaintance* can be somewhat negative and is usually reserved for someone we have met only briefly or someone we know but don't particularly like. In many other countries, the term *friend* is reserved for a few very close individuals with whom you might share the majority of your social activities. You may find yourself disappointed when your new American friend has a different idea of how much time you should spend together.

Personal Questions

Conversational questions may seem to you both too personal and too numerous — especially when you first arrive. "What do you do (for work)?" "Are you married?" "Do you have children?" (and, if you do have children, "How many do you have?") "Do you play golf? What is your average?" These are not personal questions by American standards. They are a search for common ground on which to build a relationship or base a conversation. Such questions are meant to be friendly; the person is interested in you and is not prying into your private life, at least not deliberately. These questions can also be viewed as *status* questions. Your answer to "What do you do?" tells the questioner whether you have a high-status occupation or a lower one. Married people are not necessarily higher in status, but they are often approached quite differently than single people in terms of the kinds of events to which they might be invited. Remember that what is considered personal varies across cultures.

Asking questions is how we become acquainted with one another. Since many of us move around the country so often and meet so many people in the course of a year, we tend to make quick assessments of each other. By rapid questioning we decide whether we wish to establish a relationship, because we know that in this fluid society we don't have time to learn about each other more slowly.

In less mobile countries people operate differently. They tend to protect their privacy at first, and to hold off any moves toward intimacy until there has been adequate time to assess the newcomer. Only then do they feel comfortable discussing anything as personal as their children, where they live, or what they do at work. The difference is more of timing than of intent. Americans move faster, living like a movie played at double speed, because tomorrow they may be transferred across the country or you may go back across the sea.

To those coming from countries where introductory amenities are normally handled over a longer period of time, the American way can seem threatening in its personal intensity; yet, even Americans avoid certain subjects that are considered too personal and therefore impolite. These include questions about a person's age, financial affairs, cost of clothes or personal belongings, religion, political views, love (or sex) life, and about why you don't have children or why you are not married. Paradoxically, however, such intimate questions (and even unsolicited answers!) are not unusual among complete strangers if there is little or no chance of a future meeting. Don't be surprised, for example, if a seatmate on a long bus, train, or airplane trip reveals intimate details of his or her life.

If someone asks questions that seem to you to be too personal, there are ways you can avoid answering them. You can simply smile and pleasantly turn the questions aside by a comment such as "I'll tell you some other time" or "I'd rather not say," then quickly change the subject. The American will get the point but not be offended.

Terms of Address and Titles

The whole matter of titles and forms of address may be quite strange to you. Americans have little feeling for rank, especially social rank, and few enjoy being treated with special deference to age or position (even fewer would admit it); special treatment makes them uncomfortable. Many Americans find even the titles "Mr.," "Mrs.," "Miss," or "Ms." stiff and formal. You hear people well beyond middle age say — even to quite young people — "just call me Sally (or Henry or Don)." Being on first-name terms is taken as a sign of acceptance and friendliness.

Most often introductions begin with first names: "Mary Smith, this is John Jones." This leaves the option open to you; you can call the woman "Mary" or you can call her more formally "Ms. Smith," whichever you prefer. Sometimes both of you might use the formal address for a few minutes, and then one or the other will say, "Please, just call me Mary." If you don't want to use first names so quickly, just don't. Nobody will mind.

"Ms." includes both unmarried and married women. Since men are not identified by whether or not they are married, some women feel there is no reason why they should be. "Ms." is more common in writing than in speaking. When it is spoken, it is pronounced "mizz," although some people seem to think that it is not very easy to say. Some women still accept the traditional titles of "Miss" and "Mrs." and even prefer them, but don't be surprised if you meet women who do not.

You may notice that when Americans speak together, they seldom use these titles unless they are followed by family names, as in "Mr. Johnson," "Mrs. Gray," or "Ms. Wilkins." We have no exact equivalent of "Monsieur," "Señor," "Mademoiselle," or "Madame" in conversation, as in "You're looking very well today, Mr." It would be very unusual to hear "Good morning, Mr." or "How are you, Mrs.?" If you are accustomed to hearing such forms of address interspersed throughout a conversation, their lack of use here may feel cold, impersonal, even disrespectful at first. Feel perfectly free to drop in your own "Monsieur" or "Señora" if you want to do so. It will sound interesting or different, even a bit flattering to the American! But do not be offended if we don't do it too. In the American south, "Sir," "Miss," and "Ma'am" are sometimes used in ways that approximate "Señor"/"Monsieur," "Mademoiselle"/"Señorita," or "Madame"/"Señora." In most of the country, however, these titles are considered to be too formal for everyday usage.

Because class differences are minimized in this country, we do not have inherited titles such as "Lord" or "Count" or "Duke" for distinguished people. We do, however, use certain occupational titles that recognize a status that has been earned, not merely inherited. Occupations that most frequently carry titles include diplomats, governors, members of Congress (or other top government posts), judges of the courts, military officers, medical doctors, professors, priests, rabbis, and Protestant clergy. Examples would be Ambassador Jones, Senator Smith, Governor Russell, Judge Harley, General Clark, Dr. Brown (medical), Dr. Green (Ph.D.), Professor Harkins, Father White, Rabbi Cohen, or Reverend Thomas.

Generally speaking, men in all other occupations are addressed as "Mr.," women as "Miss," "Mrs.," or "Ms." If in doubt about how to address someone, never hesitate to ask. For example, you might say, "Is it *Mrs.* Smith?" or "Is it *Dr.* Long?" If you are embarrassed about asking, yet want to be respectful, you can always use "Mr." or "Ms." Those you address will probably realize your dilemma and help you by telling you the proper title.

Unless you are distinguished by your occupation, you will find that formalities in address are quickly lost because a friendly, informal relationship is more important to Americans than either rank or status is. We can still respect a person even if we call him Charlie or Pedro. To us, informality does not mean lack of respect.

There are other American customs that visitors who are accustomed to considerable attention and service in their home countries may find insulting at first. Some may feel that insufficient deference has been paid to them in relation to their position when they are treated like everyone else in the United States. In such cases, some cultural adjustment will contribute a great deal toward a positive experience here.

A Do-It-Yourself Society

Because the United States is intentionally egalitarian, whoever we may be — lawyer, professor, bank president, or corporate executive — we generally carry our own bags, do our own laundry, stand in line at the grocery store, or shine our own shoes. Anyone who can afford the high cost of service in this country, and wants to pay for it, may. But there is absolutely no social stigma in doing one's own daily chores, no matter how menial. In fact, most Americans take pride in do-it-yourself accomplishments and may devote a great deal of their leisure time to projects around the home. Huge warehouse stores like Home Depot and Lowe's that cater to do-it-yourself projects, from building a deck to remodeling a kitchen or bathroom, have been built throughout the country.

Many Americans who can afford household help or a driver or a gardener do not employ them. They prefer family privacy, independence, and freedom from responsibility, all of which are at least partially lost when one has help in one's home. For the most part, household help has been replaced by easily operated appliances, prepared or packaged foods, wrinkle-free fabrics, and other labor-saving developments. This doesn't mean that no one employs domestic help; increasingly, even middle-class people hire a nanny, cleaning person, gardener, and/or landscaper for a few hours per week, especially in the case of single-parent families or if both adults in the household work full-time. As documented by editors Barbara Ehrenreich and Arlie Russell Hochschild in their book *Global Woman: Nannies, Maids, and Sex Workers in the New Economy,* an influx of refugees and economic migrants is altering the self-reliance that many Americans have known.[1] Many middle-class Americans are taking advantage of poor immigrants and refugees willing to work at lower wages. It is important to remember that people employed in this service industry and their employers are subject to the same government and business regulations as anyone else in a job. Employees are required to pay taxes on their salaries and share payments to Social Security with their employers. Service jobs, such as a cleaning person or a gardener, are jobs like any other to Americans, with wages sometimes equal to those of office workers, clerks, or waiters. As in other areas of life here, Americans who employ household help often attempt to treat them as social equals, insisting on being called by their first names, and making requests rather than giving orders. (See Chapter 18 for more information on hiring household help.)

Challenging Authority

In much of the world, authority is not challenged, either out of respect or out of fear, or sometimes because a hierarchy of rank has been fixed for so long that people have been trained for generations never to challenge it.

Americans are trained from childhood to question, analyze, and search. "Go look it up for yourself," a child will be told. In many schools tasks are designed to encourage the use of a wide range of materials and individual thinking. An assignment to write a paper on the world's supply of sugar (or the gold standard, or Henry VIII, or Peruvian art) will send even a young child in search of completely unfamiliar information. From the primary grades onward, children are taught to use libraries and the Internet, and to search for new ideas and information. By the time they are teenagers, some young and talented scholars are making original and valuable contributions in all fields of science, from astrophysics to oceanography. Industry is so aware of this untapped resource that each year, through national competitions, it offers awards to teenagers in order to seek out (and later employ) young people with brilliant, inquiring minds. The expression "Question Authority" has so long been the motto of American youth that in graffiti it is sometimes met with another written phrase, "Why?"

As seen by members of some other nations, this emphasis on questioning and searching is inappropriate. Visitors from other countries often feel that our youth lack respect. Newcomers are often startled and frequently annoyed to find junior staff members daring to challenge older executives or argue points with them; they do not always like it when these young men or women make often revolutionary suggestions. An executive's own blueprints, reports, or analyses may be scrutinized in detail — perhaps even challenged — by a young person. This is not to be considered an insult or loss of face, nor is it an indication of "no confidence" in the executive's experience and ability.

Our whole approach to research is different. We deemphasize the personal. A person's *ideas* are being analyzed, not the person herself. To us the two are quite separate. This is how our minds work; we are seeking facts, not challenging someone as a person. Thus, even in social conversations you will find that people often argue, pick an idea apart, ask for sources, or challenge conclusions. In general, they do not mean to be rude; they are keenly interested and merely trying to explore the idea in greater depth. Americans do this more than most nationalities; however, in some cultures z(e.g., Israeli or German) many tend to challenge people and ideas far *more* strongly than do Americans, and they should be mindful of when they may be perceived as *too* argumentative. Of course, it is true that some people in any culture do not handle their knowledge and skills in appropriate ways and can be seen as rude. Egotistical or arrogant behavior is often repaid with alienation and contempt by colleagues in the same office. Thus, bright young men and women must learn to use their knowledge and skills in cooperative, beneficial ways.

Directness

Just as our degree of individual freedom sometimes seems excessive and therefore uncomfortable to many foreign visitors, non-American attitudes toward complete honesty seem insincere and uncertain to Americans.

In many countries people will tell you what they think you want to hear, whether or not it is true. To them, this is the polite thing to do. To Americans, it is considered misleading — even dishonest — to distort facts on purpose, however kind the motive. In the United States directness tends to have a higher priority than politeness. We are taught from childhood that "honesty is the best policy." In contrast, an Arab proverb suggests that while "it is good to know the truth, it is better to speak of palm trees." In Arab countries and elsewhere, courtesy, honor, family loyalty, or many other values might come far ahead of honesty if one were listing priorities. But with us, trust and truth are interrelated and very important. Saying of a person "You cannot trust him" is one of the most serious criticisms that one can make.

In view of these value differences, it is natural that misunderstandings and irritations often occur, especially in areas where being precise is important, such as in the negotiation of contracts. A foreign businessman once said, "With us a business deal is like a courtship." Americans are not usually very good at this sort of strategy; on the other hand, you can usually count on their word. You know where you stand with them. Except in advertising and in politics, they will usually not exaggerate and promise what they do not mean in order to convince you that their product is desirable. This often-repeated question of accuracy (directness) versus courtesy (saving face) leads to many misunderstandings between people of different cultures. If you are aware of the situation in advance, it is sometimes easier to recognize the problem.

Don't think Americans are being rude if we tend to speak in monosyllables or answer with a mere "Okay," "Sure," or "Nope," or if we greet you with "Hi." Our brevity is not a personal insult, although to those accustomed to formal phrases, we may seem blunt. American informality has become more desirable than formal expressions of greeting or farewell that require language based on the situation and the status of the speakers.

You may also be surprised (and perhaps offended) by the swearing and references to sex that you hear. These kinds of expressions have become commonplace, partly because recent music and movies are full of them and partly because all languages are constantly changing. You will need to develop a keen sense of observation to learn which of these expressions can be used and when they are not appropriate. When you are not sure, it is best to avoid them. And if you do not understand them when someone uses them, you can quietly ask what they mean.

Americans are sometimes blunt because of embarrassment. We often find it awkward to respond gracefully if people compliment or thank us at any length. We are likely to brush aside such courtesies because we simply do not know what to say. Thus, you hear expressions such as "Don't mention it" or "It was nothing." The intent is not to be rude; in fact, Americans probably like your courtesy and thoughtfulness but do not want to seem to praise themselves. One of the contradictions in American society is a high regard for modesty in situations such as accepting compliments but a seeming immodesty regarding one's own accomplishments when applying for a job.

Silence

Many Americans find silence uncomfortable; they will fill almost any silence that extends for more than a few seconds with "small talk," an important part of most conversations. Small talk refers to topics of conversation such as the weather, movies, books, community events, or family. After saying "Hello," for example, the next comment might be, "Beautiful weather, isn't it?" or "Did you watch the game last night?" Then the conversation continues with more small talk. Exchanges like this might be heard at parties, on the bus or subway, at school, in the supermarket, at sports events, and in department stores.

Instead of studying in silence, many students have a radio playing. Homemakers may leave the television or radio on for the "companionship" of sound, even when they are working in some other room. Drivers listen to the car radio on their way to work.

There are aspects of this American discomfort with silence that can be confusing. "Silence is golden" is a saying familiar to many visitors who study English before they come to the United States. There are times when Americans look for a quiet place — some students prefer to study in silence; some parents encourage their children to be quiet; some people do not play the car radio. Thus, everyone, American and non-American alike, must become sensitive to the desires of his or her neighbors, friends, and even strangers to fill silence at times and to be silent at other times.

Public and Private Selves

Communication scholar Dean Barnlund observed in his landmark work *Public and Private Self in Japan and the United States*[2] that cultures draw different boundaries around aspects of individuals that are public and those that are reserved for intimate friends. Often confusing to persons newly arrived from other countries is our lack of desire for certain kinds of privacy and our strong desire for other kinds. For the most part, we are not a nation of high walls and inner courts. Our lawns often join one another without fences. Especially in small towns, friends visit each other without telephoning first and sometimes enter each other's homes without even ringing the doorbell. On the other hand, many homes have security systems nowadays, which are set when people leave for work or for the evening or when they go shopping or go on vacation.

The United States is a big country. We have never lived in walled cities or had to protect ourselves from warring princes in neighboring states. During our first centuries, most of the United States was so sparsely populated that neighbors were welcomed, not fenced out. A new face or new arrival was a cause for rejoicing. In the nineteenth century, when this nation was being developed, people lived cooperatively or did not survive. They protected one another and shared their labor jointly as they cut down forests, laid railroads, roofed barns, or husked fields of corn together. They depended on each other in all aspects of life.

Out of these early days has come a heritage of openness, which reveals itself in many ways. You will feel it as you visit our homes — in living rooms, family rooms, dining rooms, and kitchens without doors or with half walls, no walls, or glass walls. If you come from a culture that values more privacy in work and living environments, you may have to get used to colleagues who wander into your office without knocking or people who forget to close your door when they leave the room, or even people who wonder why your door was closed in the first place.

The exception to this openness is that when carrying on substantive business discussions or negotiations, Americans insist on privacy. The custom of conducting business amidst jangling telephones and people entering and leaving makes Americans nervous and frustrated.

Americans also value personal privacy. We need time to be alone. We live in small family groups; each person considers himself or herself a separate individual. Children are provided with their own private rooms if possible, where they like to go and close the door. In many cultures wanting to be alone is a sign that something is wrong. Not so among Americans, who will often resist the constant companionship offered by friends and acquaintances from elsewhere. When you come to live in the United States, you will find that after an initial welcome Americans will tend to leave you alone unless you ask for help or seek a closer relationship.

Social Distance and Touching

Anthropologist Edward T. Hall observed in his book *The Hidden Dimension*[3] that all human beings have a "comfort zone" regulating the distance they stand from someone when they talk. This distance varies in interesting ways among people of different cultures.

Greeks, Arabs, and South Americans, for example, normally stand quite close together when they talk, often moving even closer as they warm up in a conversation. Americans find this awkward and often back away a few inches. Studies have found that we feel most comfortable about twenty-one inches (53 cm) apart. In much of Asia and Africa there is even more space between two people in conversation. The matter of space is nearly always unconscious, but it is interesting to observe.

The comfort zone also applies to the closeness with which people sit together, the extent to which they lean over one another in conversation, the way they move as they argue or make a strong point, or their behavior in crowded situations. Americans, for example, try to keep their bodies apart, even in a crowded elevator.

Although Americans have a relatively wide comfort zone for talking, they often communicate with their hands — not only with gestures but also with touch. They may put a hand on a person's shoulder to demonstrate warmth of feeling or an arm around a person in sympathy. They may nudge someone in the ribs to emphasize a funny story, pat an arm in reassurance, or stroke a child's head in affection. They readily take someone's arm to help him or her across a street, and they often hug one another in greeting or farewell. To many people — especially those from Asia — such body contact is unwelcome. Southern Europeans and Latin Americans, on the other hand, tend to see us as cold because we gesture and touch so little compared to them.

Americans in Motion

Americans are a restless people. Many of us travel whenever we get the chance, and although most of us do not leave the country, the family vacation is an annual tradition. Highways are jammed with cars, especially on holidays. We also crowd onto trains, buses, and planes. In increasing numbers, we hike with packs on our backs or ride bicycles, heading for the mountains, seashore, or national parks. Americans are joined by millions of tourists from other countries who come to enjoy the people and the culture. Don't be surprised if you are crowded and jostled by throngs of travelers, Americans as well as those from all over the world.

The adage, "Don't just stand there, do something!" implies that doing anything at all is better than doing nothing. Granted, many of us waste far too many hours watching television, but it would be unthinkable for most of us to lie on the couch without the TV or a book to give us a sense of doing *something*. Just as we have a low tolerance for silence, doing nothing at all often makes us tremendously uncomfortable.

As discussed in Chapter 1, we are a mobile society. Our ability to move across the country, where we have no friends or family, may seem baffling to many visitors (although perhaps not to you, having come all the way to this country). Moving is extremely common, as is the freedom people have to reinvent their identities when they do so. People change their names, their religions, and very often attempt to change their economic status along the way.

Controlling Nature

Many people in the world — Asians, for example — seek a balance with nature. Many Americans try instead to control nature. We speak of harnessing a river, conquering space, taming the wilderness. Asians (and many others) think more in terms of compromise, consensus, or harmony. Americans believe anything can be done if we just put our minds to it. "The difficult can be done today; the impossible takes a little longer." So the searching, challenging — sometimes arrogant — mind goes to work.

Fortunately, we are beginning to realize that we cannot control nature. We are coming to understand how we have wasted, spoiled, and polluted for the sake of transient gain. We are worried now about the nation's resources, our environment, and our health. You will read about this in our newspapers and hear it discussed widely wherever you go.

Personal Progress and Changing Jobs

In many parts of the world, personal influence is almost essential in getting ahead. One needs a godfather or a sponsor. Here, that is not usually true. Naturally, all people use influence sometimes, but one rarely advances far on that basis alone in the United States. Here, traits that lead to success are generally considered to be willingness to work hard (at any kind of job), scholarship or skill, initiative, and an agreeable personality. In other words, even in the area of personal progress, this is a do-it-yourself society. By and large, success is neither inherited nor bestowed. This means, therefore, that our employment practices are different from those in many other countries.

In some nations it is considered disloyal to quit a job; deep reciprocal loyalties exist between employee and employer. Lifelong job security and family honor are frequently involved. But in the United States, Americans consider "job hopping" a characteristic of our mobility. We consider it a right to be able to better ourselves, to move upward, and to jump from company to company if we can keep qualifying for better jobs.

This constant changing of personnel seems unreasonable to many citizens of foreign nations: "Where are your roots?" "How can you be so cold and inhuman?" "You act as if you are dealing with machines, not humans." They do not understand that a great many Americans *like* to move about. New jobs present new challenges, opportunities, friends, experiences, and often a new part of the country.

The employer may be quite content, too, when someone leaves a job. Perhaps he or she has had the best of that employee's thinking; a new person may bring in fresh ideas, improved skills, or new abilities. Then, too, a newcomer, lacking seniority, will probably start at a lower salary. Changing jobs is so readily accepted here, in fact, that good employees may bounce back and forth among two or three corporations, being welcomed back to their original company more than once through their career, each time at a higher level.

Materialism

Status symbols such as cars, high-definition plasma televisions, and swimming pools often confuse visitors to the United States. Some cultures are accustomed to a system in which a luxury market supplies a small number of expensive goods for the rich; everyone else does without. In the United States this is less true. Because our economy operates on the basis of a mass market, blue-collar workers, miners, farmers, even people on welfare own goods that represent great wealth in some other countries. In terms of hours of work required to buy such luxuries, the cost is low. Secretaries, high school students, bank tellers, clerks, or janitors can and do buy cars, take vacations, and own all kinds of luxury items. Often they purchase these things on the installment plan, and the costs over a reasonable period of time are not prohibitive in terms of their wages. In fact, many items considered a luxury abroad are assumed a necessity here.

This difference can be perplexing for the visitor who, understandably, interprets wealth in his or her terms, thinking a Cadillac or membership in a golf club must indicate upper class and education. As a result, the visitor expects to find that the owner possesses the status that accompanies the leisure class in the visitor's country. This is not necessarily so. We do seem to acquire a great many *things,* even though in many cases they are not necessarily of great quality. One fast-growing segment of television programs and magazine articles is on the subject of managing all the things we acquire. A new industry in storage containers, and a growing occupation of professional organizers, help the American whose penchant for buying new things exceeds his or her ability to keep track of them. Some people are so completely overwhelmed by the things they own that there is even a diagnosable mental condition for people whose compulsive buying habits interfere with normal functioning. This is not an affliction of the wealthy only. There is such an availability of cheap goods in discount stores that even the working class can buy more than they can use. In addition, as the more disciplined among us attempt to reduce our belongings by selling them at garage sales and yard sales (not to mention moving sales — remember how mobile we are!), others of us acquire box upon box of books, magazines, records and tapes, compact discs, home movies, clothing, gadgets, knick knacks, even appliances such as televisions, air conditioners, and computers by shopping at those sales!

As you will no doubt soon learn, one primary cause of this endless materialism is advertising. The expression "keeping up with the Joneses" is a common way to express the effect of our neighbors' spending habits on our own. For example, if Jill Jones, our neighbor, should buy a new car, ours will seem less adequate by comparison. Similarly, if she installs a pool or enlarges her home, we will feel an urge to do the same. In her book *The Overspent American: Why We Want What We Don't Need,*[4] Boston College economist Juliet Schor explains that one problem today is that we no longer compare ourselves to our neighbors (in fact, we rarely know our neighbors or their spending habits well enough to compare ourselves with them). Instead, mass advertising through television has created a world of fictitious Joneses for us to try to keep up with. "When poet/waiters earning

$18,000 per year, teachers earning $30,000 per year, and editors and publishers earning six-figure incomes all aspire to be part of . . . one referent group, which exerts pressure to drink the same brand of bottled water and wine, wear the same . . . clothes, and appoint their apartments with the same . . . furniture, those at the lower economic end of the reference group find themselves in an untenable situation." You will probably stare in wonder at the size of vehicles many Americans drive — sport utility vehicles (SUVs) — while complaining about gasoline prices that may well seem strangely low to you, particularly when compared with other commodities.

The size of the average new home has doubled in the past fifty years — another symptom of what John De Graaf, David Wann, and Thomas Naylor dubbed, "affluenza" in their recent book of the same name.[5] After all, we need bigger homes to store all of our new material goods.

There are, of course, social and economic (as well as environmental) costs to all of this buying. The older, depression-era saying "waste not, want not" is rarely heard any more. Things are bought and discarded with little thought to the impact of those decisions, and this is surely a phenomenon that will need addressing in the future.

Parochialism

Because of our country's large geographic size, many of us feel that there is enough here to keep us occupied without looking for adventure abroad. It has been estimated that around 20 percent of U.S. Americans own a passport. If you consider that many of those are naturalized citizens who obtain a passport primarily to travel to their home countries, the number of U.S.-born citizens with passports is even lower. Evening news broadcasts on the major networks rarely contain any news that isn't directly related to the U.S. or our interests. We are a country full of people who know little about the rest of the world. Very few U.S.-born citizens can speak another language, and languages are not even offered in most public schools until the age of 11 or 12. Very few people, even college graduates, are ever required to study even a year of a foreign language.

It is possible that this is changing. After September 11, 2001, and the subsequent wars in Afghanistan and Iraq, more Americans are realizing that there are consequences to an insular view of the world. Interest among university students in studying abroad is increasing as never before. The

BBC World News is available on my National Public Radio stations, cable and satellite television, and on the Internet. Government agencies, especially in law enforcement but also in other areas, are recognizing the importance of having employees who are linguistically and culturally literate in another country's ways. Businesses in this era of globalization are seeking managers and executives who can thrive in an overseas posting.

On the other hand, some Americans have a renewed desire for isolationism, some because they are afraid our policies will cause more violence toward the U.S., and others because they feel less desire to help those in other countries than before. Whatever the reasons, the unfortunate fact remains that many of the Americans you will encounter will be woefully uninformed about the rest of the world. You may feel slighted that your American colleague is unaware that your country is the cultural capital of its region or that it has any number of distinctions, but try not to take this too personally. You will find that despite our ignorance, many of us are eager to learn from you.

As with any generalization, be careful not to stereotype. Many of us are in fact well-read in world affairs, have traveled or even lived abroad, and can indeed speak another language.

3

American Cocultures

In addition to the dominant American culture, it is important for you to understand other cultural groups — also called *cocultures*. The long-cherished American notion was that this nation was a great "melting pot," meaning that cultural differences were eliminated by the blending of different ethnic groups. In fact, this is a myth; the U.S. is not a melting pot at all, and never really was. This is a reality underlying the fast-shifting social patterns of today. There are still many U.S. Americans of European descent, however, who cling to this notion and resist the idea of cultural diversity. They maintain the belief that many of their ancestors shed their own cultural patterns, adopted English as their language, and became "Americans." This way of thinking, called *minimization* by intercultural relations theorists, minimizes the importance of cultural differences and emphasizes the commonalities. While this can be attractive for those whose cultural norms dominate cultural institutions, it is often resisted by cultural minorities who would like to see their own norms and values reflected in the country's educational system, political life, and workplaces.

The early settlers in this country were mostly white Anglo-Saxons, and most of them were Protestants, sometimes referred to (derogatorily) as WASPs (White Anglo-Saxon Protestants). As you can see by reading American history books, the contributions made by many incoming groups — Africans, Latinos, Catholics (mostly Irish and Italian), Japanese, and Chinese — have long been overlooked. At first, members of these groups worked hard to become assimilated where possible — that is, to become a part of mainstream culture. But for a large proportion of these groups, assimilation has not been possible. For many people, it is not even considered desirable.

As the years have passed, the proportion of white Anglo-Saxon Protestants to other culture groups has declined, and in some places (especially large cities) whites have become a minority. According to the U.S. Census bureau, white people who are not of Hispanic* origin (i.e., not from Puerto Rico, Mexico, or Central or South America) comprise 69 percent of the overall U.S. population (down from 83 percent in 1970). Latinos make up 13.5 percent of the overall population, African Americans 13 percent, Asian Americans and Pacific Islander Americans 4 percent, and Native Americans (including American Indians and Alaskan Natives) about 1 percent.[1]

In addition to racial and ethnic diversity, consider that there were nearly fifty million people in the United States living with a disability, or almost one in five persons. Finally, one of the most dramatic changes in the U.S. population has been an increase in the foreign-born population (immigrants and refugees). The populations of a few small cities near large metropolises are now 50 or even 70 percent foreign born. Clearly the social issues, both positive and negative, involved in such a shift of ethnic groups present a major challenge to the United States.

There is currently considerable discussion as to how much bilingualism — mainly English and Spanish — should be allowed or encouraged in schools, government documents, and election ballots. The United States does not have an official language, but there is political momentum to establish one: English. The perception is that many people are refusing to learn English. The reality is that for most immigrants, the first generation learns little of the new language, but their children (second generation) are bilingual and bicultural, and their grandchildren (third generation) know almost nothing of their grandparents' native tongue.

Ethnic Differences

The growing minorities, having been rejected over the years, are understandably turning to their own ethnic and racial backgrounds, seeking

---

[1] "Hispanic," like most terms that attempt to categorize people, is hotly contested. The term preferred by many is "Latino," but "Hispanic" here is used to maintain consistency with the Census Bureau's nomenclature.

their own group pride and identity out of their own past histories. In general, Americans who are not of European ancestry are from a group that is less individualistic than the dominant culture. This fact makes it more difficult for many whites to appreciate the strong notions of family and group identity held by many members of other groups.

The problems of ethnic conflict in American society have been so played up in the world's media that visitors to our shores are often surprised when they see blacks and whites working side by side in offices, factories, schools, and institutions in cities across the country, and when they notice that close friendships exist across ethnic lines. Keep in mind, however, that many places in the U.S. are not well integrated; the majority of ethnic group members (including European Americans) tend to live in communities where they are a majority.

Many *people of color* (the currently preferred term to refer collectively to people whose ancestry is not primarily European) arrive in the U.S. fearing varying degrees of discrimination. Slights, insults, and narrow-mindedness do still exist, unfortunately, especially in the crucial areas of housing, schools, and jobs. There are still frictions and sometimes riots, and educational equality remains a dream. There are also areas of the country where people of other ethnic backgrounds do not enjoy the full range of opportunities available to whites.

Real friendships between races, full trust, and easy social encounters are not yet the norm. However, barriers continue to be broken down, especially among younger people.

Nondominant groups in the U.S. can be described not only by race and ethnicity; disability, age, and sexual orientation all influence the cultural identities of their members. It is also important for visitors to keep in mind that members of nondominant groups may feel that their identity is either primarily with their ethnic group or with the larger American population. In other words, they belong to both groups. Culturally, many are able to shift back and forth between the dominant culture and their original culture and may be more comfortable with one or the other, or equally comfortable with both. In addition, intercultural marriages are leading to a multiplicity of cultural identities. It is no longer unusual to meet someone whose ancestry reflects any combination of African, Asian, Caribbean, European, Latino, or Native American influences. The next sections briefly explore the largest of these cocultural groups in the United States.

African Americans

Because the mass media have concentrated mostly on the negative, with little reference to any kind of progress, newcomers to the U.S. may at first be surprised at the economic range they will find among African Americans. Education has opened the way to better jobs. Black executives, judges, elected officials, and professors are no longer rare. More and more African Americans are buying houses and apartments in middle- and upper-class neighborhoods. Integration varies by locality, and progress is slow, but in the past fifty years there has been much forward motion.

Black visitors from abroad will experience varying degrees of acceptance, depending considerably on their own educational background, economic status, and personality as well as on the local environment in which they find themselves. Many black visitors do not experience the same levels of prejudice as do African Americans. Your special status as a foreign student, professor, businessperson, and so on often leads people to behave with more deference than they might toward a local person. It is also true that many African Americans are more aware of minor acts of discrimination than you would be able to perceive immediately.

In most places, you do not need to fear violence or personal attack because of your race or ethnicity. Sadly, of course, there are exceptions to this. In the United States, as in every country, there are places where extra caution is needed. It is a good idea to discuss your concerns with a local colleague for guidance about which areas to avoid, especially at first.

Because many African Americans are descended from slaves, they are sometimes thought of as "involuntary immigrants." Interestingly, many recent Caribbean immigrants, also descended from African slaves, do not in general identify themselves as African American, in part because they came to the U.S. willingly.

African American identity is complex. Culturally, African Americans often show markedly different patterns from those of European Americans. For example, titles are more widely used among African Americans, and first names are more often reserved for close friends and family of similar age. In addition, many interpersonal conflicts between whites and blacks are the result of different patterns of emotional expression, according to researcher Thomas Kochman.[2] With whites, showing anger by raising one's voice is sometimes a prelude to a physical fight, while among blacks emotional authenticity in discussion is perceived as honesty.

Many people believe that African Americans should assimilate and would do so if racial barriers were eliminated. Others believe that the African American culture and heritage are too important to sacrifice. The ascendancy of modern African American cultural achievements, such as art, literature, and musical forms like rap, hip-hop, blues, and jazz shows that complete assimilation is not necessary in order to achieve social and economic prominence. But as a society we still have a long way to go, and African Americans (especially men) are still overrepresented in prisons and underrepresented in our universities. Some progress is being made, and black visitors will encounter much goodwill, acceptance, and friendship among both African Americans and members of other groups.

The first holiday in honor of an African American, civil rights leader Martin Luther King Jr., is now celebrated nationwide each January, and February is Black History Month. Kwanzaa, a modern holiday that incorporates religious tradition with African history, is increasingly celebrated throughout the country.

Latino Americans

In terms of actual numbers, Latino Americans are the fastest-growing group in the United States as well as the largest minority group. Latino Americans consist primarily of people of Mexican heritage, followed by Central and South Americans, and they live mostly in the West, Southwest, and Midwest. Puerto Ricans[†] are concentrated largely along the east coast, especially in New York, but they are moving in greater numbers into the Midwest; and many Cuban Americans have settled in Florida. The political violence in Central America in the 1980s brought countless more immigrants from El Salvador, Guatemala, and Nicaragua. Latinos add a special blend of Spanish, Indian, and African cultures to the national fabric, bringing with them the heritage of the Caribbean and various parts of Central and South America. A Mexican man talks of the Latino heritage in the U.S. in a speech:

[†]Note that residents of Puerto Rico, a U.S. territory, are citizens of the United States.

We explored and charted areas and regions which, for example, later became Florida, Georgia, Louisiana, and Missouri. We were the first cowboys. Through our ancient knowledge of irrigation we made an oasis out of desert areas in Arizona and California. We built many of the waterways, railroads, and charted many of the original trails that became the highways of the southwest.

— Gilbert G. Pompa, former Director of Community
Relations Service, Pontiac, Michigan

The number of Latino Americans grew by 60 percent in the 1990s. The numbers of Latino Americans are now so great (nearly 39 million in 2003, about 13 percent of the nation)[3] that you will find bilingual (Spanish-English) schools as well as signs and instructions in many parts of the country. Bilingualism, especially in the schools, is an issue of some significance in the United States and supported by many people. Others feel that efforts to provide public school instruction in a student's first language (not only Spanish but other languages as well) subvert the "melting pot" vision of American society and sow the seeds of disunity. Thus, you may encounter the "English only" debate, especially in newspapers, where national policy on the subject is discussed.

Latino Americans are considered by many to be "sleeping giants" on the political scene. Although their political influence is not yet commensurate with their numbers, they are beginning to realize that they have the potential for power in the political arena. California, Texas, Arizona, and New Mexico all have large Latino populations, which is not surprising given that Mexico's borders extended far enough north to include all of those States (and part of Oregon) until just over 150 years ago. This has led to the observation on the part of many Mexican Americans that "we didn't cross the border, the border crossed us." As noted earlier, Florida and New York also have large numbers of Latinos, many from Cuba and Puerto Rico, respectively. Latinos have been appointed to national political offices and judgeships; they have been elected to state and national legislatures and governors' offices.

Like African Americans, Latino Americans often exhibit markedly different cultural patterns from those of European Americans. For example, titles are widely used among Latino Americans and first names are more often reserved for close friends and family of similar age. Many Latino Americans are also more status-conscious than their Anglo counterparts are, and they have a higher respect for authority and hierarchy. Punctuality tends to be less rigidly adhered to, and relationships are highly valued. Finally, the family unit remains much more tightly knit in many Latino families, and there is a much greater emphasis on the extended family than within mainstream families.

Asian Americans

Four percent of the U.S. population is of Asian origin, concentrated most heavily in California and Hawaii but also in New York, Boston, Minneapolis, Houston, and Chicago, and Asians are now scattered increasingly throughout the country. Most live in and around large cities. For many years, the immigration laws of the United States imposed strict quotas on immigrants from Asia, resulting in slower growth in their numbers compared with other immigrant groups. The Chinese Exclusion Act of 1882 was repealed in 1943, but it was not until the immigration laws were completely revised in the 1970s that things really began to change. Our past race-conscious policies also influenced immigration patterns — for example, U.S. citizens of Japanese ancestry were held in special prison camps during World War II, while German Americans and Italian Americans remained free.

Many Asian Americans are Indochinese refugees, called by some "a caste of survivors" because of the ordeals they experienced in leaving their countries. For the most part they have great family cohesiveness and a deep respect for education. A smaller but growing proportion of Asians is from the subcontinent (India, Pakistan, Bangladesh, and Sri Lanka) or the Philippines.

A far larger number are of Chinese, Japanese, and Korean origins; for this group the Confucian ethic is still a strong factor in their behavior. "In that ethic," says sociologist William Liu, "there is a centripetal family orientation that makes people work for the honor of the family — not for themselves. The Confucian ethic is very compelling — as was the Protestant ethic in the days of America's founding fathers — a great motivator."[4]

The high value that many Asian Americans place on education has resulted in a disproportionate number enrolling in the nation's most competitive universities: Harvard, Massachusetts Institute of Technology (MIT), University of California at Berkeley, University of California at Los Angeles (UCLA), and many others. This in turn has given rise to the stereotype of a "model minority" group, which, although a positive stereotype, can be just as harmful and no more accurate than negative stereotypes about any ethnic group.

U.S. immigration policy, which favors the highly educated, has resulted in a "brain drain" to the U.S. Asian engineers, doctors, and scientists have been coming to the states in greater numbers in recent decades. Among the best known have been I. M. Pei, the architect, and An Wang and Samuel Ting, Nobel laureates in physics. The United States has also been greatly enriched by many other Asians who are successfully competing in a variety of fields.

Native Americans

As a percentage of their own population, American Indian and Alaskan Native peoples are the fastest growing population in the U.S., according to the 2000 Bureau of the Census. The number who declared themselves at least partly Native American in combination with other races grew by 2.2 million, an increase of 110 percent, while the number who declared themselves only American Indian or Alaskan Native grew by more than 500,000 in 2000, or 26 percent. Of course, some of this increase represents a rise in self-reporting, rather than a change in birth rates. The sad fact remains that these increases are overshadowed by the prior decimation in the population of the country's first peoples — down from at least 12 million before the arrival of the Europeans in the fifteenth century.

There are more than five hundred recognized and unrecognized tribes in the United States. Today, the largest tribes include Cherokee, Navajo, Choctaw, Sioux, and Chippewa. Most Native Americans live in the western part of the United States. Alaskan Native groups include the Inuit and the Aleut. Many Native Americans live in self-governing communities called "reservations," while others live in mixed communities throughout the country. Native American tribes are independent nations, governed by treaties with the United States.

Native Hawaiians and other Pacific Islanders also comprise an important group of indigenous peoples. There are nearly 500,000 of them, nearly half of whom live in Hawaii and California. Although lacking the political status (i.e., sovereignty) of Indian tribes, Native Hawaiians are a potent political force, and there is a movement to regain recognition as a sovereign people. This movement is, of course, quite controversial, and it is difficult to predict what will result from it.

Native cultures often contrast sharply with the dominant American culture. Honoring elderly people, living in harmony with nature, connecting with family, appreciating silent reflection, and a nonlinear understanding of time are all common among native peoples. The most common opportunities for interaction with Native Americans is through the many resorts and casinos operated by various tribes throughout the country. Because of their unique political status, Native Americans have found it easier than other people to obtain licenses for gaming, resulting in a large number of casinos operated by the various tribes on their own land. This has been the source of considerable political controversy, pitting anti-gambling interests against those of both the gaming industry and those who believe that Native Americans have received such poor treatment from our government over the centuries that they should have complete self-determination rights whenever possible. Especially in the American West, tribes often offer tourist visits on their land. These can range from stereo-typed "re-creations" of a long-gone way of life to multi-day hosted events, which can help bring outsiders closer to Native Americans and their issues.

Other Groups

The diversity of Americans is not limited to our ethnicities. Retired people, gays, lesbians, bisexuals, and people with disabilities have formed political, cultural, and even residential communities.

Retired People

The American Association of Retired People (AARP) is one of the largest and most influential political groups in the country. Claiming over 60 million members, politicians take their views seriously when forming or changing legislation. Retirement communities, especially in Florida and Arizona, are among the fastest-growing categories of real estate. In much of the country, there are special social and recreational events, and even dating services catering to the over-sixty crowd. Many U.S. Americans encourage their elderly parents to move into a retirement home or assisted-living facility. Because most households are either single-parent or two-career couples, many people believe that their elderly parents will be better taken care of in such a facility than at home. Too, many elderly people do not wish to burden their adult children, many of whom are raising their own children. Still, it is not uncommon for elderly people to live with their children in their old age, as is more common in much of the world.

Americans with Disabilities

The United States has an estimated 54 million people with a permanent disability, nearly 20 percent of the population. *Disabled* doesn't only refer to physical differences. Millions of people are affected by mental illnesses and learning disabilities ranging from schizophrenia and manic-depression to attention deficit/hyperactivity disorder. There has been a tremendous shift in public understanding of mental illness in the past few decades, and while still difficult, all but the most severe of these cases are treated with the goal of helping the disabled person be an active member of society.

As in many other countries, people with disabilities are an important political and cultural force. Deaf people, for example, often participate in a distinct culture that is not easily accessible to the hearing. Since 1992, the Americans with Disabilities Act has created a powerful force for making sure that our public spaces, businesses, and educational institutions are accessible to everyone. There are wheelchair versions of most sports, and clubs, interest groups, and social organizations especially for people with disabilities are thriving. Of course, participation in the larger society is encouraged and common as well.

Because education is compulsory to age 16, young people with disabilities can put a tremendous strain on the educational system. Public schools are often criticized for spending a large amount per student with limited results, but the reality is that a significant amount is spent on students with special needs, making it appear that all students are direct beneficiaries of public expenditures. See Chapter 19 for more discussion of the educational system and its pressures.

Advances in emergency medical treatment mean that many severe and profound injuries that would have been fatal a decade ago are now resulting in a permanent injury. There are roughly 2.4 million disabled veterans from the armed forces. While new military technologies mean that fewer service personnel than ever are killed in action, the ratio of those who are permanently wounded to those who are killed has risen dramatically. Advocates for people with disabilities often point out that this is the one minority group that anyone can join without warning. While there is certainly considerable room for improvement, the United States has become one of the most welcoming countries in the world to people with disabilities.

Lesbian, Gay, Bisexual, and Transgendered Americans

The term *lesbian* refers to a woman with a homosexual orientation, and *gay* usually refers to a homosexual man. However, the term *gay* is also used for both men and women. Transgendered people are those whose biological sex is different from their social gender, meaning that a man is living as a woman or vice versa. Modern American history of gay (homosexual) rights began with a riot in New York City in 1969. The "Stonewall" riot, named for the bar where it occurred, was a result of a concerted attempt on the part of the police to harass gay and lesbian people. They did this by posing as homosexuals and arresting those who made sexual advances to them, which was then illegal for same-sex couples. Gays and lesbians, tired of being harassed, rose up to proclaim their rights as equal citizens. As one of his first official policy initiatives, President William Clinton proposed ending the ban on gays in the military, in a compromise that pleased neither side of the debate: the "don't ask, don't tell" policy. This policy made it acceptable for a gay man or lesbian woman to be in the armed forces, as long as no one knew about it.

As a country, we have come a long way. The United States may appear to be something of a gay heaven if you are in San Francisco or New Orleans and are from a country where gays dare not be identified as such. On the other hand, if you are from northern Europe and are in a small American city, you may be shocked at how repressed the gay environment is. Like many societies, the U.S. has no singular viewpoint on homosexuality. There are now gay characters on television shows, and the popular "Queer Eye for the Straight Guy" highlights the widely held belief that gay men are knowledgeable about fashion and style, and heterosexuals can benefit from their advice. And as mentioned later in Chapters 4 and 7, there has been a recent movement to recognize gay marriages in some parts of the country. At the federal level, however, the ironically named "Defense of Marriage Act" frees states from recognizing marriages performed in other states, and this is aimed specifically at preventing the spread of recognition of gay marriages. The American Episcopal Church has its first openly gay bishop, although the resulting tumult and strongly conflicting opinions may well divide the Church into two separate organizations.

There are, sadly, still incidents of violence, including murders, directed at individual gay people. In general, gays and lesbians are not protected by law from discrimination, but of course enjoy the same protections as other people. By and large, many organizations and businesses — including more than three-fourths of Fortune 500 companies — include sexual orientation in their own nondiscrimination policies, and public harassment is generally not tolerated.

Class

Americans like to claim that we are a classless society. A large middle class, a high standard of living, mass-produced clothing, deliberately casual speech, and the wide use of first names all combine to give the nation a classless appearance, especially to newcomers. But under this superficial appearance of equality, Americans are, in fact, quite conscious of class differences.

In fact, University of Pennsylvania English professor Paul Fussell writes in his witty book *Class: A Guide Through the American Status System*[5] that there may be as many as nine distinct social classes in the United States! He places these into three categories: top "out-of-sight" class, upper class, and upper-middle class in the first category; middle class, high-proletariat, mid-proletariat, and low-proletariat in the second category; and destitute and bottom out-of-sight class in the third category. While these nine classes are more fanciful than they are sociological constructions, Fussell's observations resonate easily with many observers of American life.

In 2003, according to the U.S. Census Bureau, one-fifth of American households earned less than $18,000 per year, and one-fifth earned more than $83,000. Five percent took in over $150,000. It is important to remember, however, that in the United States people can, and do, move from one class to another on their own merits (or misfortunes). To move up to a higher status, a person needs enough energy, determination, and ability to be successful at something. He or she can start as a salesperson, factory worker, taxi driver, or bank teller. Americans respect — and many are themselves proof of — the "self-made individual." You can hear these kinds of success stories all around you if you ask people about their youth: the woman whose father was a miner and she is a leading journalist, the man who put himself through school by selling brushes and is now president of the brush company. These are the dramatic success stories, but for every one who gets right to the top, there are thousands of others who, less dramatically but nonetheless truly, climb beyond their parents on the social, educational, and economic ladder. Conversely, of course, there are those who move down.

This flow of people from one social level to another indicates that in the United States, both the word and the idea of class mean something quite different than in many other countries. Not only is this nation made up of highly diverse ethnic, racial, and social strands, its inhabitants are also enormously mobile geographically. People move from one location to another with remarkable frequency as they search for ever better employment. One statistical study reports that one out of five families moves every three years.

This ceaseless mixing and merging into new communities, this repeated adjustment to new environments and people are important factors in trying to understand the baffling question of class in the United States. The do-it-yourself, independent, questioning American personality is another factor.

In many countries, a person's social position is still a group matter, shared with the family, the wider group of relatives, perhaps even the whole village or district. In the United States, however, position in society is, at least to some degree, personal rather than determined by family or group.

Before World War II, the extended family unit in the United States was stronger than it is now. Uncles, aunts, grandparents, and children of all ages vacationed with one another, came together for holiday festivities, and were closely knit. But as economic development has taken hold, social patterns have changed. The talented mathematician, scientist, or manager is suddenly in great demand and often moves quickly to higher levels of status and wealth. Expanding companies transfer their employees to new locations, removing them from stable family ties; more and more people settle in small houses or apartments in urban areas where grandparents and other family members can no longer share space.

The same shift is beginning to take place even in developing countries. Nowadays one who can read and understand the newspaper or fix a tractor may, and often does, take over from the traditional leader. Technology puts a premium on youth. Skilled young people move ahead, starting their families in new ways and locations, often giving up traditional values and customs. As the "onward and upward" restlessness becomes more and more widespread, class structures are torn apart by the force of twenty-first-century demands.

Frequently, it is just one member of an American family who surges ahead, becoming president of a university, head of a firm, or a well-known member of government while the rest of the family remains in modest jobs in a modest environment. When new frontiers beckon, many Americans may feel no sense of commitment either to their relatives or to their community. They may come back now and then to their former environment, but many move away, never to return. Others, of course, maintain strong ties of affection and loyalty.

For most people class is a complex and changing concept. Class boundaries, therefore, overlap considerably. Studies show that four out of five Americans, when asked, describe themselves as middle class. In most other countries higher percentages of people tend to define class more precisely and therefore describe themselves as either upper class, upper-middle, or lower-middle class, or lower class. Nowadays, American social and class structure is undergoing profound change. As the United States continues to move from an industrially based society to one based on electronics and information, the traditional blue-collar middle class is disappearing. Some worry that as the trend toward downsizing, computerization, and out-sourcing continues, the middle class will shrink as many displaced workers are forced into low-paying service jobs.

Success can be defined as that which gives a man or woman more status than he or she possessed before. It can be won through skill, intelligence, leadership, and sometimes sheer perseverance — regardless of birth. In the American scene, success has normally been accompanied by increased financial resources. Upward-moving people, therefore, have found themselves associated with first one and then another success level, with its accompanying financial status.

As a result, success and class in the United States are determined both by a person's job and by his or her pattern of consumption. Since class is a flexible, competitive state, people try to make their position clear with visible and recognizable symbols such as cars, houses, club memberships, vacations, and so on. Those who have remained on the same rung of the social and economic ladder are often subtly rejected by those who have risen.

Racial and ethnic discrimination should be seen in this country against the background of a much broader (but less discussed) tendency of many Americans to exclude one another — of any ethnic group — through fear of losing their own place. Prejudice here is in fact often more economic than racial, though racial prejudice is a constant source of conflict that thoughtful people continually try to eliminate from society.

Class and status are, in the end, difficult even for Americans to interpret. No one will expect you to do so. However, if you can understand that in the United States social position is not a stable, inherited factor, you will comprehend much about this nation.

Part II

American Institutions

4

American Social Life

Americans lead active social lives, and it can be puzzling for new-comers to learn our customs for forming and maintaining relationships. This chapter explores some of the norms of making friends, socializing, and dating. Participating in an active social life will no doubt be one of the most rewarding — and at times frustrating — parts of your American experience.

Friendships

In this mobile society, friendships can be close, intense, generous, and real, yet fade away in a short time if circumstances change. Both parties may exchange holiday greetings for a year or two, perhaps a few letters for a while, then stop. If the same two people meet again by chance, even years later, they often pick up the friendship where they left off and are delighted to do so. This can be perplexing to those from countries where friendships develop more slowly but then become lifelong attachments, with mutual obligations, extending sometimes deeply into both families.

In the United States you can feel free to visit people's homes, share their holidays, and enjoy their children and their lives without fear that you are taking on a lasting obligation. Do not hesitate to accept hospitality even though you cannot reciprocate. Americans will not expect you to do so;

they know you are far from home. Americans will enjoy welcoming you and be pleased if you accept their hospitality.

Another difficulty for many people from other countries is that although Americans include them warmly in their personal everyday lives, they do not demonstrate a high degree of generosity if it requires a great deal of time. This is the opposite of the practice in some nations, where people unstintingly give of their time to someone but do not necessarily admit him or her into the privacy of their home. In some countries hosts will appear at airports in the middle of the night to meet even a casual acquaintance; they put their car at the visitor's disposal; they take days off to act as guides — all evidence of impressive generosity. But these same people may never introduce their wives or invite the guest to participate in their family life. In both cases the feeling is equally warm; the pattern of expression, however, is different.

Distances, pace, and the pressures of life are tremendous in the United States. Also, without household help, cooking, cleaning, baby-sitting, and other domestic responsibilities must be absorbed into each person's day (as well as all professional, community, and social demands). As a result, many Americans will extend their welcome warmly at home but truly cannot manage the time to do a great deal with a visitor outside of their daily routine. We will probably expect you to get yourself from the airport to your hotel by public transport; we assume that you will phone them from there. Unless you are chairman of the board or a similar dignitary, you may be expected to find your own way (by cab) from the hotel to the host's office (or home). However, once you arrive there, the welcome will be full and warm and real. Most visitors find themselves readily invited into many homes here. In some countries it is considered inhospitable to entertain at home, offering what is considered "merely" home-cooked food, instead of doing something special for a guest. Restaurant entertaining indicates more respect and welcome. Also, for various other reasons such as crowded space, privacy, language difficulties, or family custom, outsiders are not invited into homes in many other countries.

In the United States entertaining at home and at a restaurant are both common, but it is often considered more friendly to invite a person to one's home than to go to a public place, except for purely business relationships. The farther one is from big cities, the more likely this becomes. So if your host or hostess brings you home, do not feel that you are being shown inferior treatment.

Don't feel neglected if you do not find flowers awaiting you in your hotel room either. This happens graciously in Thailand, the Philippines, the Caribbean, the Netherlands, and many other countries where flowers are inexpensive and plentiful. Flowers here, though, are exceedingly expensive, hotel delivery is uncertain, and arrival times are often delayed, changed, or cancelled — so flowers are not customarily sent as a welcoming touch. Please do not feel unwanted! Outward signs vary from culture to culture; the inward welcome is what matters, and this will be real.

Parties

Among the more interesting customs to observe as you travel the world are the ways in which people conduct themselves at parties. In some countries men and women drift to opposite ends of the room and talk to one another; in others they sit in large chairs around the edge of the room and talk only to the people on either side of them, or they may silently eat and observe the scene. It is normal in some countries for people to remain patiently silent until introductions have been made, then to talk only to those to whom they have been properly introduced.

When you first arrive at a large party in the U.S., the host (this term refers to male or female) may introduce you to two or three people nearby, but if others are still arriving, he or she may then leave to greet newcomers, expecting you to go on by yourself, introducing yourself as you move about from group to group. If this feels too uncomfortable, it is quite all right to say to someone, "I am a stranger here and do not know anyone. Could you introduce me to some of the people?" Most people will feel flattered that you turned to them for help and will gladly escort you around the room, introducing you and easing your discomfort.

Americans move about a great deal at parties. At small gatherings we may sit down, but as soon as there are more people than chairs in a room — or better yet, a little before this point — you will see first one and then another make some excuse to get up (to fetch a drink, greet a friend, or get something to eat) until soon everyone is standing, moving around, chatting with one group and then another. Sitting becomes boring beyond a certain point. We expect people to move about and be "self-starters." It is quite normal for us to introduce ourselves; we will drift around a room, stopping to talk wherever we like, introducing ourselves and our companions. If this happens, you are expected to reply by giving your name and introducing the person with you; then the men, at least, generally shake hands. Sometimes women do so as well. A man usually shakes a woman's hand only if she extends it. Otherwise, he just nods and greets her.

After such an informal introduction, you usually talk together for a little while. Here are some of the inevitable questions you'll be asked, probably by several people: "Are you new here?" "How long have you been in America?" "Did you bring your family with you?" "What do you do?" (referring to the sort of work you do). Within a moment or two, you will hopefully have found something to talk about and the conversation will move along for a while. Then either person can feel free to say something informal like, "Well, it's been nice to meet you" or "I hope to see you again soon." This is the signal for both people to move to another group.

The basic rule at big parties is this: don't stay in one place too long. Pick out people you think look interesting, then go talk to them. The point of a party in this country is to meet and talk with people; the fact that you are all there together under your host's roof is in itself a form of introduction, in our view. As a result, anyone can feel free to talk to anyone else.

Our easy come-and-go pattern is unfamiliar to people from many other countries. Like much else about the United States, it stems in large measure from our size, our numbers, and our constantly shifting population.

Invitations

You should answer any written invitation as soon as possible. Some will have R.S.V.P. (a French abbreviation meaning "Please reply") written at the bottom. Such invitations require an answer, but even if such a request is not included, it is still a courtesy to let the host know whether or not you expect to attend. If a telephone number is given, you can phone; otherwise, it is best to write a short note, either accepting or expressing your regrets. Often invitations come by e-mail (or include an e-mail address), so an e-mail reply is fine.

It is perfectly acceptable to decline an invitation, written or otherwise, although this is one area where a "white lie" — a harmless lie to protect someone's feelings — is usually preferable to the truth. You can say, for example, "I'm sorry, but I have another commitment that evening," and unless you are already good friends with the host, he or she will probably not pry into what kind of commitment you have. It is not considered polite to accept an invitation unless you actually plan to attend. On the other hand, if you are not sure you will able to attend, you may usually be noncommittal.

Many invitations will be in person or by an informal telephone call. When accepting an invitation, always make it a habit to repeat four things: (1) the day of the week, (2) the date, (3) the time, and (4) the place. You may say, for example, "Let me make sure I have the details right: Tuesday, January 11, 7:30, at your home." Then you are sure you have understood correctly.

If you do not know how to get to the host's home, this is the moment to ask for directions and to write them down. A good way to make sure you have the directions correct is to repeat each phrase as the host says it (for example, "Turn right on Broadway"), and when the directions are completed, repeat all of them once more. You might also ask your host to e-mail the directions, or you can use the Internet to obtain driving directions from your address to the party.

Since telephones are so widespread that communication is easy in the United States, it is considered rude to accept an invitation and then not appear without phoning your regrets *in advance.* If something prevents you from attending, you should always telephone your host immediately, just as soon as you know you will not be able to go. Briefly explain the circumstances and express your apologies. The host may want to invite someone else in your place, or, if you are the guest of honor, he or she may change the date of the party to suit your schedule.

Announcements

Much social life in this country takes place at communal parties of one kind or another — group activities sponsored by a church, a school, a company division, or a club. These may be dinners, picnics, tours, weekend camping or skiing trips, lectures, concerts, receptions, bowling evenings, or any of a wide variety of affairs. If you have some connection with the sponsoring group, you can assume that you will be welcome to join in any such gathering. Many others are open to you whether or not you have a connection. If you see a poster, read a notice, or find a note in the newspaper announcing an event, don't wait to be invited. Just go if you wish; no one else will receive a personal invitation either. The announcement may read "Open to the Public." Such community affairs are friendly and an excellent way to meet new people. If in doubt as to whether or not you would be welcome, just ask someone, but do not feel hesitant just because you were not specifically invited. If it is a cooperative party, do your share of the work and participate in the fun, too. Sometimes these events are "potluck," meaning everyone brings a dish or two to add to the food being served; sometimes there is a charge to participate; sometimes everything is free.

When to Arrive and Leave

For Meals.   You should arrive at the time indicated in the invitation or within five to fifteen minutes after that time. If you are very early, walk around the block or wait in your car or downstairs in the lobby. In this country the host and/or hostess are also likely to be the cooks. Give them time to do last-minute preparations; don't arrive early. On the other hand, if you find you are going to be more than twenty to thirty minutes late, it is a courtesy to your host and hostess if you telephone and tell them so. They may turn off the stove and be grateful to you for not having spoiled a meal by your lateness.

For Cocktail Parties, Receptions, Teas.   Invitations for formal events usually say "from X hour to Y hour" — 5:00 P.M. to 7:00 P.M., for example. This means that you can come any time that suits you between those hours. You do not have to leave exactly at the time indicated, but you should go within a half hour of the end at the latest. Following the example of the other guests is a good policy for newcomers.

For a Dance.   Most people arrive thirty minutes to an hour after a dance starts. There is nothing more dreary than a dance that has not yet gotten under way, unless you are a true dancer who likes the floor uncrowded and the band fresh.

For Concerts and the Theater.   Plan to arrive at least ten minutes before curtain time, or much earlier if the event is to be "general seating," which means that no seats are assigned ahead of time. You will want to take off your coat, read the program, and settle down before the play or concert begins. In many theaters and concert halls, if you are late you will not be seated until the first break in the program. Also, you should plan to remain until the very end of the program, or if you must leave early, do so during an intermission. Unlike in some countries, live performances bring with them the expectation that the audience will not interfere with the enjoyment of others.

For Weddings, Funerals, Public Lectures, Sports Events.   Be there about ten minutes before the specified time so that you will be seated and relaxed by the time it starts. In some cases you will want to arrive earlier to get a good seat.

For Business Appointments.   Arrive exactly at the moment of an appointment or a few minutes early. It is considered a discourtesy to keep a busy person waiting. If he or she keeps you waiting, however, try not to show impatience. The person whose office is the scene of the meeting takes precedence. If you do not want to give him or her this advantage, arrange to meet in your office or on some neutral ground such as at a restaurant or in a hotel lobby.

Drinking Alcohol

Drinking habits vary widely among Americans. Some families never serve any alcoholic beverages. Others have cocktails before dinner, wine with the meal, and/or after-dinner drinks. If you are not accustomed to American cocktails, be cautious; they are often quite strong. Women as well as men drink alcohol, but you should not feel any hesitation in asking for a sherry, Dubonnet, or nonalcoholic drink (such as Coca-Cola or fruit juice) if you do not want a cocktail. In some homes the cocktail hour may become quite lengthy. If it does and you do not wish to have more than one drink, it is perfectly all right to refuse. You can also drink as slowly as you like. Eating some of the food that is offered with the drinks is a good idea; these snacks may be cheese and crackers, olives, peanuts, potato chips with creamy "dips," or other small "finger foods."

If the host asks, "What will you have to drink?" you can reply, "What are you serving?" or you may request a particular drink if you prefer.

Common cocktails offered in most homes include the following:

- *Gin and tonic:* a particularly popular summer drink made with gin, quinine water, and ice — often with a sprig of mint and a slice of lemon or lime.

- *Scotch or bourbon:* two types of whiskey, served with water or with soda or "on the rocks." This last phrase means simply that liquor is poured over ice with nothing added. You can ask for "on the rocks with a little water" if you want the whiskey somewhat less strong.

- *Martini:* colorless but powerful; made with dry vermouth and gin, served either on the rocks or "straight up," meaning no ice is included. Martinis are served with a twist of lemon or an olive. You may also ask for a vodka martini.

- *Manhattan:* sweet and dark-colored, made with sweet vermouth and whiskey, served either on the rocks or straight up.

- *Bloody Mary:* a mild drink, often offered before lunch or at brunch (a meal combining breakfast and lunch served late morning), made of spiced tomato juice with a "shot" (one to two ounces) of vodka or gin, served over ice.

- *Screwdriver:* vodka and orange juice, also often offered at brunch. Some people drink these for cocktails, served over ice.

Drinks served on ice are not quite as strong as drinks served straight up, especially after the ice has melted a bit. Americans use more ice than almost any other people in the world.

Many people prefer beer or wine instead of a cocktail, and most homes that serve cocktails also have beer and wine available. You can ask for white wine or red wine when the host asks you what you would like.

When office colleagues stop for a drink together on their way home, the one who made the suggestion often pays for the first drink; the companion frequently offers to pay for a second. There are no hard-and-fast rules, though; they may each pay for their own. Normally, if someone says, "How about a drink?" each pays his or her own bill. Many people have a drink over a business lunch. If you do not want to do this, you can certainly decline. Beer or wine is also often ordered at lunch.

Do not be surprised if you are offered coffee, tea (iced or hot, depending on the season), or even soft drinks with a meal. Water is not always served, but feel free to ask for it in either a home or a restaurant.

Dinner in a Home

Dinner with Americans in their homes is likely to be informal and relaxed. You will probably be served family style. Platters and bowls will be passed from person to person, or the host may serve from one end of the table. All ages eat together. There is no clear division of labor in many modern American families. Serving cocktails, preparing dinner, clearing dishes from the table after the meal, washing dishes or putting them in the dishwasher — any of these chores might be done by one person or by several members of the family. Whether or not you help with any of these chores will vary depending on your rank and age, how often you have been to the home, and family custom. If you are a homestay student or a long-term visitor, you will come to be treated as part of the family and will participate in these responsibilities. If you are a visiting businessperson or executive, or other special guest, you will not be expected to participate. In general, people who "roll up their sleeves" and help with these chores, or at least offer to do so, are thought of more highly than those who appear to be treating the host or hostess like a servant. At a minimum, it is usually good form to help with "clearing the table" or bringing the dirty dishes from the table to the sink area.

At meals, it is the custom to wait for the host to begin eating and to finish as closely as you can to when everyone else does. Watch your host from time to time to judge your own speed. Americans tend to eat rather more quickly than many other people; you may be embarrassed if you find yourself far behind everyone else at the end of the meal.

If for religious (or other) reasons there are some foods you cannot eat, explain in advance to your host when the invitation is extended. You may say, "I should tell you that I do not eat pork for religious reasons," or "I'm on a rather restricted diet on the advice of my doctor, who tells me I shouldn't eat meat," or "I'm a vegetarian, and I hope this doesn't cause you any inconvenience." If you were unable to explain in advance, you can do so after you are at the table and see that there is something you shouldn't eat, or you can just leave it on your plate uneaten. Even though at first American food may be different and you may not enjoy it, it will please your host if you eat at least some of every dish and express appreciation for the effort. The cook (or cooks, since both husband and wife may have participated) in the family will probably have tried very hard to please you.

The American habit of shifting the fork from right to left hand when the knife is used — then back again — is unfamiliar to many. Don't feel you must struggle with this awkward custom. Do whatever is comfortable for you. It is usually not considered correct, though, to soak up gravy with bread or to tuck your napkin under your chin, although some Americans do these things. Watching your host is a good idea! It is almost never appropriate to make any kind of slurping, burping, or other noises while eating at the table. You should not smoke at the table unless your host or hostess does; otherwise, you can ask if there is a place for you to do so. (See also "American Food Habits" in Chapter 13).

You will naturally thank a host as you leave, but if you want to be considered really polite and pleasant, send a note within a day or two after the event. This will be greatly appreciated. If you prefer, you can express your thanks by telephone instead. This should be done on the day immediately following the party. Not everyone does this, but it is not difficult, and the host family will remember your gesture for a long time.

Buffet Meals

"Buffet" meals (in contrast to "sit-down dinners" are a popular means of entertaining because they are informal and easy to manage, even without household help. There are no exact rules about what is proper; your host will indicate how people should proceed and where they are to sit. You can probably figure out what to do by watching other guests. Systems vary from household to household, depending on the way the house is arranged, how many people there are, and so on. The point is for people to feel at ease and to have a pleasant, relaxed time together.

Pot Luck

An extremely popular form of entertaining, especially among young and single people, is the "pot luck" dinner. In this style, each guest is responsible for a different portion of the meal. For example, one person will bring a salad, another the entrée, a third a side dish, and a fourth dessert. Often these meals are "themed" — Middle Eastern, Mexican, Chinese, etc. You may well find that the theme is food from your country — try not to take offense if someone makes your national dish unrecognizable!

Bringing Gifts

Bringing flowers or a small gift when you are invited for lunch or dinner is always welcome and gracious, especially when you first visit and on special occasions such as a birthday or Christmas. We go in and out of each other's houses so informally and so often, however, that gifts are by no means an obligation. If you do bring something, it should be small and simple — a gesture rather than a gift — perhaps a bottle of wine, a souvenir from your country, a small box of candy, an inexpensive bouquet of flowers, or something equally modest. If you are going to be an overnight or weekend guest, it is customary to bring a present, still not elaborate but perhaps more special than a gift brought for only a meal. Remember that lavish gifts often make us uncomfortable.

Relationships between Men and Women

Americans are still trying to work out the meaning of equality between the sexes, and some men are confused about the changing roles or even threatened by women who are assertive and who hold administrative and executive positions. This is a difficult time for men who have traditionally felt that they should be breadwinners and women should be homemakers. In general, however, a cultural adjustment is taking place, and most people realize that men and women can actually get along on an equal footing with one another.

Courtesies between the Sexes

In spite of the movement toward equality, many women still appreciate some traditional courtesies and will not be offended by them, and many men still want to extend these courtesies to women, particularly in formal situations. In most cases, men may still open doors for women and stand back to allow them to go through first. Women in the United States usually walk ahead of men into a room or theater or restaurant.

Adult Dating

Men and women go out together a great deal, especially in the cities. They ski together, work together, and dine together, either at restaurants or in each other's apartments. A date does not mean that they are necessarily interested in having sex together, though it may appear so and, of course, with some men and women, it is so.

If a man invites a woman to a restaurant, she will not feel that she owes the man sex because he has paid for her dinner. She will feel that her company and her acceptance of the man have contributed toward a pleasant evening for both but not that she owes him more. Men cannot buy sexual intimacy by offering a woman a meal or gifts.

American women are accustomed to easy companionship and equality. Anyone who comes here expecting to find American women meek, obedient, or submissive is likely to have a hard time. Today's American woman is very much her own person: independent and intending to stay so. She expects to make her own choices and expects decisions to be made jointly.

Who pays for dates? A general rule of thumb is that a woman in business or college will pay her own way during the day. "Going Dutch"* (meaning that each person pays his or her own expenses) is common, although if a man asks a woman on a date he should offer to pay. If, however, a man asks a woman to something special outside normal working hours — for cocktails or dinner, a dance, or the movies — the invitation itself means "Come as my guest." The whole matter of dating is in transition. Young men and women are quite open and candid in talking over who will pay and for what. You can feel free to ask your friends for advice in your situation.

Single Women

A woman can go alone into a restaurant for breakfast, lunch, or dinner, but most usually avoid sophisticated, expensive restaurants in big cities or fancy nightclubs with floor shows and/or dancing. Single women also usually avoid public bars, unless they are with a friend or go to one of the many bars catering to singles, but they can go comfortably to cocktail lounges in hotels.

In today's world it is generally advisable for a single woman not to hold a sustained conversation with a single man who approaches her in any public place in one of the large cities. A few words and a smile are fine, but if a man pursues a conversation, he may well be looking for a "pickup," meaning an easy date for sex. Avoid letting him see or overhear your address or room number until you get to know him well.

---

*With apologies to those from the Netherlands, but this is a common, if unconsciously pejorative, expression in the United States.

Single men and women coming to a job in the United States will often have to work a bit at finding ways to meet people for possible friendships or for dating. Men and women in offices are likely to be family people who rush out at five o'clock to get back home to their spouses and children. Single poeple often fear developing an intimate relationship with someone they will see and work with every day. There is also much discussion nowadays about sexual harassment in the workplace, as discussed in Chapter 8.

If you are a single woman, the best way to meet men — or other women, for that matter — is likely to be through sports activities or some kind of club or organization. Go skiing or join a bowling team; play golf or tennis; take a membership in a swimming or aikido club. If you are less physical, sing in a chorus, join a book club, or enroll in an evening class that appeals to both sexes — pottery, photography, or ballroom dancing, for instance.

If you are asked for a date, remember that you can set the pace. In this country the man sometimes does the inviting and the planning, but he is likely to find out first what will please his guest. You will probably have an opportunity to indicate the kinds of things you enjoy: hiking or listening to music, being with a group or eating alone together by candlelight. In addition to choosing along such lines, it is you who also sets the level of friendship. You can keep things platonic if you want to. If the man seems increasingly affectionate and you want it to be otherwise, you can make that clear. The woman has the choice.

It is perfectly acceptable for you to invite a single man to dinner or a party, either alone or in a group, although it is unwise to accept a date with a stranger. Also keep in mind that to a single man, an invitation for drinks in your apartment can sometimes be interpreted by the man as an invitation for sex as well.

Single Women and Single Men

Most big cities contain many single men and women who come from elsewhere to work. Since both find it hard to meet new people, many "singles clubs" have sprung up. These can be free-for-all places to pick up someone for sex, or they can be extremely nice clubs, offering theater parties, cocktail parties, and other activities to help men and women become acquainted. These organized clubs sometimes publish a monthly booklet or have a bulletin board describing the range of activities that will take place that month. If you are interested, you can go to whichever parties or events you choose. If you find congenial people of either sex, that is fine. If not, you may try again on some other occasion. There are always people at the door to introduce you and make it easy for you to meet and mix, even if you are alone.

Start slowly if you join such a group. Be a little reserved and cautious at first. The super-friendly type who rushes up to make friends may in fact be the club bore looking for a new audience. Give yourself time to look over the situation before you become too friendly with anyone. Clubs of this sort are often found through religious contacts or affiliations; otherwise, ask around or watch the local newspapers.

There are also a large variety of sports/exercise clubs that cater to men and women, married and single. These clubs can be a nonthreatening way to meet someone while doing something you like.

Personal advertisements, or "personals," have become a very popular way for single men and women to meet. It is particularly attractive to those for whom the club or bar scene isn't appealing. Most daily and weekly newspapers as well as many magazines offer personals, with numerous formats and response setups. You may either respond to an ad or write your own. These services are usually quite reasonable compared with expensive dating services.

Internet personals have become extremely popular, and this popularity has largely removed the social stigma once associated with personal ads. Although often quite expensive, Internet matchmaking services offer the convenience and security of screening its subscribers, but you should of course remain cautious.

Arrange personal meetings in public places and refrain from giving out your address or workplace information until you have a chance to get to know the person well. Matchmaking services are also increasing in popularity. Innovative approaches such as "speed dating" parties have also gained in popularity. In this arrangement, each person gets a set number of minutes to spend individually getting to know a number of other people. If there is mutual interest, longer dates are then arranged.

But *shopper, beware!* Responding to personals can be dangerous, especially in large cities. Discuss this with colleagues or friends before taking any chances; there may also be some listings that are less risky than others.

Sexual Relations

To many men of the world (including some American men), the fact that a woman will readily go off alone with them often seems to imply that she is sexually available. This is not true, and it is important to realize this from the start. You will scare off many American women if you rush in too fast; they may seem very friendly yet have no intention whatsoever of having sex with you at the first meeting or, for that matter, at any other time. Most American women are not promiscuous. They may choose to have sex, even extramarital sex, but generally not unless they feel real affection for the man; and most stay with one man at a time for considerable periods. Most are not looking for "an easy score" and do not appreciate the assumption that they are.

If you have a wife or husband at home, be sure to let this fact be known to your acquaintances early on. It will not necessarily make any difference, but we want to know your situation. We will feel tricked and will frequently cut off the relationship immediately if suspecting that the other has cheated, lied, or otherwise been misleading.

In general, men dating American women should generally not make any move toward having sex on the first date, or the first several dates. In today's world of free speech you can ask a woman how she feels about having sex, but your chances will be poor if you move too fast too soon, regardless of how casual things may look.

Another important thing to keep in mind is the legal implications of pursuing sex too aggressively. In most states, sex can be legally considered to be rape if it occurs without the consent of both parties. Thus, if your date does not consent, or is unable to give consent (e.g., if she is incapacitated by alcohol or other drugs), she may press criminal charges *even if rape was not your intention.* Although direct communication about sex and sexual interest is difficult (even for most Americans, despite our direct style of communication), it is essential to avoid misunderstandings, which can have devastating consequences.

Gay and Lesbian Social Life

In most cities there are bars and restaurants catering to gays and lesbians. If you are gay, lesbian, or bisexual, you may find listings in the telephone directory for a gay and lesbian community center or service center, which will provide information on local bars, organizations, or clubs. Also, one can often find newspapers and magazines in large bookstores that will list establishments catering to gays and lesbians.

Recently, some states and municipalities have started granting marriage licenses (or their equivalent) to gay and lesbian couples, sparking a national debate that should prove interesting for some time to come. Depending on how things turn out, you and your partner may find yourselves taking the opportunity to get married! A note of caution, however, if your partner is a U.S. citizen or permanent resident and you are not. It will probably take quite a long time for immigration law to "catch up" with gay marriage, meaning that such a marriage will not have the standing of a heterosexual marriage in terms of extending residence to you. Entering into a gay marriage might even be construed as evidence that you are no longer intending to be a "temporary" visitor, which can cause problems in renewing visas or extensions of stay in the future.

As in any country, the questions of when, whether, and to whom to "come out" to are difficult to answer. Certainly many people are "out" in their public lives, and others remain "in the closet," meaning that they prefer to keep their sexual orientation private. Perhaps the majority of gay and lesbian people choose a balance, keeping their sexual orientation private at work while remaining open about it in their social lives. Sadly, there is still discrimination against gay and lesbian people, although it is often less obvious and blatant than it once was. Learning to read the cues of acceptance in your new environment will be key to a comfortable adjustment to the United States.

5

American Civic Life

As a democratic, free society, the United States depends heavily on the involvement of its citizenry. Civic obligations include more than just voting, although only about half of all eligible voters do vote. Most Americans also volunteer their time and money to a myriad of charitable causes, including their religious group, social service agencies, neighborhoods, and communities.

The American Political System

Those who come from nations where the national government is centralized and strong may find personal involvement in politics baffling. "Grassroots democracy" seems to them chaotic; the relationship among our cities and towns, counties, states, and the nation is hard for them to understand.

To a U.S. American, the word *state* means one of fifty geographic and fairly autonomous entities, united somewhat loosely by our federal government. But to a Syrian, a North Korean, a Paraguayan, or many others, a state may mean a strongly centralized national government with absolute powers far beyond those held by our federal authorities. To those accustomed to this sort of rule, centralized governmental power is normal and feels comfortable. Such people expect a leader to act decisively, quickly, and alone. They may have a hard time understanding the American preference for compromise, committee decision, or consultation with many people, some of whom may, in fact, be the leader's political enemies. Long delays and legal or political quibbling while our government "tests the winds of public opinion" are often mistakenly interpreted as meaning that our government does not really care about the question or is, in fact, not sincere in its stand.

What newcomers need to understand is that Americans recognize differences and allow leeway within (1) the law, (2) policy, and (3) the actual situation. These three factors often pull and tug just as a ship creaks and strains when its hull meets conflicting winds and waters. But it remains a ship, and it continues to move ahead, however slowly. It does this because it has play in its joints. Therefore, like the ship, the country does not sink but can stay afloat even under heavy stress.

Let us look at the deeply divisive national problem of civil rights:

1. *The law:* By federal law there is now neither legal nor constitutional discrimination against anyone because of race.

2. *Policy:* The federal policy states that discrimination is illegal and should be phased out "with all possible speed." (On the other hand, so-called "reverse" discrimination in the form of affirmative action is still permissible, although the allowable forms are still hotly contested.)

3. *The facts:* All too slowly, with uneven pace, sometimes two steps forward and one step back, faster in some states than in others, the United States is making attempts to end racial discrimination against minorities as well as against those with disabilities.

The country has been struggling for a long time with countless other serious issues that occur at national, state, local, and personal levels, gradually working out accommodations and resolving various kinds of problems. Despite deep regional, emotional, and personal differences, the nation is kept on course throughout this process by the law of the land.

It is often difficult for those from highly centralized nations to understand, but the fact is that final power really *does* lie in the hands of the people in the United States. This is true whether one speaks of political, economic, or social power. Americans distrust and will not long tolerate being pushed by an authoritarian leader or government. They want to keep power decentralized; they like it that way. Social issues such as civil rights, illegal immigration, divorce laws, equality of pay for women, abortion laws, gay and lesbian rights, and health care are therefore hotly debated for a long time at both the state and national levels. National law reflects many state differences and attitudes. Change comes slowly, after endless debate. But those changes that finally become the law of the land mostly do so eventually with the consent of a nationwide majority. Thus, most laws remain stable once in place.

Majority-Minority Politics

The fact that a member of a minority group will usually accept the outcome of a hotly contested election peacefully, and the idea of cooperation among bitter political adversaries are difficult concepts for many visitors to understand. Some people fear what legal scholar Lani Guinier called a "tyranny of the majority," meaning that in our system, 51 percent of the votes yields 100 percent of the power.[1] Unlike in many countries, here the legislature is not apportioned among all of the political parties receiving a minimum number of votes. Rather, each seat is voted on separately, and the candidate with the most votes in his or her district wins. Indeed, in such a system, it is difficult to imagine how minority voices are ever heard in the political system. In the presidential race of 2000, George W. Bush had fewer popular votes than Al Gore did, yet ultimately became president through our Electoral College process. Although presidential races have been decided by the Electoral College in the past, this was the first time in over a hundred years that this has happened. The Electoral College is designed to prevent a candidate from becoming president with the support of only the most populous states. The interesting thing for the visitor to note is that despite its many twists and turns, for all its passionate partisanship, the election of 2000 shows just how stable the system really is. In the end, most Americans accepted the outcome without major strikes, protests, or riots.

Americans start early to learn the political system. Sometimes, even in first grade, they campaign, vote, and elect class committees and class officers from among their own number. Or the teacher will appoint children to the "Fruit Juice Committee," "Goldfish Feeding Committee," "Blackboard Cleaning Committee," or similar rather strange-sounding committees, found even as early as in kindergarten classes. The process of voting, the notion of responsibility, and the idea of "majority-minority" soon become familiar to young Americans. They learn to accept defeat and work toward another day — to live, in other words, within our type of governmental structure.

The American Way of Giving

Americans are highly motivated to contribute financially to causes in which they believe. Thus we give generously to colleges and universities; hospitals and other nonprofit institutions; charitable, religious, and relief organizations; and environmental groups.

The American system of private philanthropy parallels our system of private enterprise. Huge trusts and family foundations provide millions of dollars annually for charitable causes. In addition to those large donors, however, millions of individuals make direct contributions to charities. Thus, schools, businesses, factories — almost any place where there are employees — encourage people to contribute to one cause or another. One of the best-known methods is through the United Way, an umbrella organization that collects contributions and then distributes them in the form of money, clothing, or food to various worthy causes. Offices have "drives" of a week to a month during which the employees try to raise a certain amount of money, their goal for that particular year.

In addition, many organizations raise money through direct mail (or telephone) appeals. Letters from those organizations arrive in the mail often, and individuals choose which ones, if any, they will send contributions to. No one is obligated to contribute, but many people do, to whatever extent they are able.

Throughout the year, but especially at Thanksgiving and during the holidays, charitable organizations collect new or used clothing, toys, and food to distribute to the poor and needy. In addition, "walkathons," "bikeathons," and "telethons" are another method of raising money for worthy causes. For example, each year many cities hold walking, bicycling, or running events to benefit research on AIDS and breast cancer. During these events, participants walk (or bike or run) a mile or several miles or even many miles in order to raise funds for AIDS victims and for cancer and AIDS research. Friends of those who participate pledge an amount of money based on the distance.

Besides wanting to help those in need, Americans are provided with tax incentives in the form of tax deductions for charitable contributions. Three out of four American families donate to charities each year. When individuals file their tax returns each year, they are allowed deductions for various kinds of charitable contributions. This is the way the American system helps charitable organizations to continue their good work.

Volunteerism

The Bureau of Labor Statistics estimates that more than 59 million Americans over the age of 16 volunteered some of their time in 2002. This represents 25 percent of the population of Americans 16 years and older. Because "Time is money," volunteering one's time is seen as even more generous than donations to charity. Americans commonly volunteer to help feed the poor and the homeless, to read books to elderly or blind people, or even to build homes for those who cannot afford to buy one themselves. Government-sponsored programs such as Americorps/VISTA (Volunteers in Service to America) attract young people eager to give a year or more of service. More than 250,000 people have served in Americorps since 1994. Numerous high schools and colleges have instituted volunteer requirements or formal opportunities, many of which are connected to the curriculum under the rubric "service learning."

6

American Religious Life

Nearly two-thirds of Americans say that religion is important to them. Despite (or perhaps in response to) the seemingly endless stream of films produced in this country that depict sex and violence, there has been an increase in religiosity among Americans. Fundamentalist forms of Christianity (those that take the New Testament more or less literally) are on the rise. The United States, for all of our emphasis on freedom of religion, is at first glance remarkably homogeneous. Nearly 90 percent of Americans are connected to some form of Christianity. Judaism and Islam, each with about 2 percent of the population, are the next largest in membership, and Islam is the fastest growing religion in the United States. Of course, these numbers mask an incredible variety within those categories. In addition, in large and even medium-sized cities, it is possible to find places of worship for most of the world's major faiths including Islam, Hinduism, Buddhism, and B'Hai. This reflects again the variety of people from all over the world who now make their homes in the United States. However, in smaller towns or rural areas, you will in all probability find only Christian churches (including Catholic and several Protestant denominations) and perhaps a Jewish synagogue. The dominance that Judeo-Christian values hold on our public discourse should come as no surprise.

Like many aspects of American culture, our feelings about public displays of religion are in conflict. Recently a judge in Alabama was removed from office for refusing to move a prominent display of the ten commandments, and that event showed Americans were largely split on the issue. A recent survey showed that while 70 percent of us prefer a president with strong religious beliefs, 50 percent are uncomfortable when politicians discuss how religious they are. The Pledge of Allegiance (to the American flag) is commonly recited at the beginning of public events. The words "under God" were added in the 1950s during the Cold War, and there has been an ever-growing controversy over whether it violates the cherished notion of the separation of religion and government. The Cold War also saw the introduction of "In God We Trust" as the national motto and its addition to the U.S. paper currency (although it was previously found on many coins). Secularism is also prominent in American public life, and in general atheists and agnostics are accepted at work or school without difficulty.

Because the American population is so mobile, we often find ourselves free to reinvent ourselves in our new location. Thus, we are culturally free to convert to different religions almost at will. It is not unusual for Muslims or Buddhists to be from Christian families. Interfaith marriages do not often result in the conversion of one spouse to the other's faith, but instead the couple might seek out a different faith altogether. Unitarian churches, for example, often have among their members Jews who have married Christians. We are even free to invent our own versions of faith, with many interfaith congregations representing a conglomeration of Islam, Judaism, Hinduism, Buddhism, and Christianity.

A hundred years ago, the various Protestant denominations were quite distinct from one another, and people rarely intermarried. After World War II, when college and university enrollment dramatically increased, the number of intermarriages rose sharply. Today it is difficult even for many Baptists, Methodists, Presbyterians, Congregationalists, and Lutherans to describe the differences among themselves. Catholicism (and the various branches of Eastern Orthodox Christianity) has remained largely distinct from Protestantism, but that distinction is now gradually becoming blurred as more interfaith marriages occur.

Especially in small towns, churches are centers for much social and community life. You will find such activities as suppers, dances, discussion groups, sports and social get-togethers, youth programs, and the like. Although you may not be given a personal invitation to these events, you will be welcome at any of them; they are held for the express purpose of including everyone in the life of the church. Most religious groups will welcome you, regardless of your faith or nationality. Churches that are identified as "evangelical" may be eager to "convert" visitors, but most will be happy just to meet you and will be curious about (and respectful of) your own religious background. There are evangelical branches of nearly every denomination, so it is important not to generalize from a few interactions. When a Lutheran family moves to a new city, they may find that the local Lutheran church is too liberal or too conservative for their taste but that the local Methodist congregation is about right — or the other way around.

In the southern states, it is not unusual for new acquaintances to ask what church you attend. This is not usually an attempt to recruit you to their faith — rather, it is a common way to discern the economic status and community another person belongs to. Because American Protestants who relocate to a new city will usually "shop around" for a church they feel comfortable in, you will probably receive many well-meaning invitations to attend a variety of churches. New friends will no doubt hope that you will join *their* church, out of the desire to ensure frequent social opportunities rather than a hope for a religious conversion.

If you do not see a congregation of your own faith near your new home, turn to the Yellow Pages under "Churches and Synagogues" (or, in larger cities, "Churches, Synagogues, and Mosques"). If you find a religious community you like and want to attend regularly, just introduce yourself to the minister, rabbi, imam, priest, or other leader — an introduction by an intermediary is not important. If you make the first move, the congregation will welcome you, help you to meet people, and assist you in many ways to settle into the community.

Many of our churches and other places of worship offer so much in the way of social life that some people find it overwhelming. You need not take part any more than you want to. People may urge you to attend a particular activity out of the desire to make you feel welcome, but if you prefer to participate only in the worship services, do not feel that you are obligated to do more. It is a completely personal choice. Among the types of activities you will find most congregations offer, in addition to the services, are nursery schools for little children, after-school programs for older children, lunches, discussion groups or voluntary work opportunities, outings, prayer or study groups, women's groups, and even singles' groups in some congregations.

Many congregations hold "coffee hours" after religious services. These are informal and friendly, and everyone is welcome to follow the group into the social room for coffee and cake or doughnuts. No one waits to be invited. It is open to everyone, but everyone is then expected to talk to people, introducing themselves, whether or not they know anyone. Have some refreshments, talk with anybody you see there, and leave whenever you want. It is a pleasant, easy way to meet people of the neighborhood and community.

7
American Family Life

With our high percentage of women in the workplace, decline in the birthrate, and high divorce and separation rates, it is hard to find the once-typical family consisting of father at work, mother in her apron at home, and two children. This profile accounts for less than 7 percent of all American families, difficult though that may be to believe. Today it is far more common for families to be headed by a single parent or for both parents to be working, managing their lives in ways unpredictable even twenty years ago.

"For us it works out well," said one father who splits house and child care with his wife, an airline flight attendant. "I know the children much better than I did, the quality of time we all spend together is better, the children have adjusted easily, and working has added an important new dimension to my wife's life."

Not all families are so liberated. The day-to-day management of families can, in fact, be quite difficult for working women who still do most of the household tasks as well, fitting them into weekends and evenings after a full day at work.

Society is groping for ways to adjust to the high number of women in the workforce. Much research is being done on the impact of this trend on the stability of families. Interestingly, to date there is no evidence of a relationship between employed women and divorce. In fact busy wives and higher incomes seem to be contributing to greater stability. Social observers who formerly predicted the decline of family life in the United

States are now revising their predictions. They say there are signs that the divorce rate is no longer climbing. More people are getting married later — with greater maturity. It is young people's marriages that are still the most likely to end in divorce. Unmarried "cohabitation" — or living together — is common now at all social levels, especially if there are no children.

There is growing recognition that the family is a diverse and complex institution, the traditional family being only one of its forms. In these days of steadily rising costs and increasing financial pressure, the family is not likely to revert to its old traditional form.

Men do a good deal more around an American house than is true in many parts of the world, especially if both husband and wife have full-time jobs. Either sex does whatever needs doing in many households — including caring for the baby, taking out the trash, and washing dishes. Men usually cut the grass and take care of major outdoor jobs, women often do the shopping, but it could be the other way around in some households. In other words, there is no clear-cut distinction between husband and wife concerning domestic responsibilities.

Women's equality with men is still a sensitive issue in the United States. Almost 60 percent of women of employment age are working, and they play prominent roles in business, political, social, educational, and community affairs. Women outnumber men in law schools, medical schools, and graduate schools in many fields. Women who work outside the home are demanding equality with men in terms of both responsibility and salary, but there is still a long way to go. Women in the professions, in offices, in shops, in factories, and in all sorts of jobs often receive salaries well below those of men for the same job. Such discrimination is illegal, but it is often difficult to prove that gender is the only reason for differences in pay. On the other hand, 30 percent of married American women with jobs earn more than their husbands. In an increasing number of American families (around 5.6 percent according to the Bureau of Labor Statistics), the husband stays home and the wife goes to work at a job. Some "stay-at-home-dads" are involuntary, the result of temporary unemployment, but many are choosing this option in light of rising childcare costs and the opportunity to be a more intimate part of their children's lives.

Some married American women still choose to be homemakers. For that matter, in today's world, taking care of all the tasks of managing a home and children is considered a vocation, and some economists have even suggested that homemakers should be paid a salary just like those who choose to work outside the home.

What's in a Name?

An increasing number of married couples are finding that the tradition of taking the man's surname (the last name) as the new family name is not desirable. Thus, it is extremely common for a variety of alternative conventions to be selected by people struggling to achieve a new level of equality. One new convention is for each adult to keep her or his own family name; the children take the father's name or a hyphenated name made up of both parents' family names, such as Smith-Jones. Sometimes, the whole family takes the hyphenated form, and in other cases, the children and mother take the father's name as their family name but the mother retains her family name as a middle name.

Future generations will have to agree on a new convention. As it stands now, if little Alonzo Davis-Keramidas grows up to marry someone named Alison Thompson-Garcia, their children might end up named Davis-Keramidas-Thompson-Garcia! A few couples are going so far as to abandon their family names altogether and creating new ones. For example, if John Goldsmith marries Lisa Schliemann, they might change both of their surnames to Goldmann. It is a further example of our willingness to sever our ties to the past and to look to the future.

Gay and Lesbian Families

As discussed in Chapters 3 and 4, the question of whether gay and lesbian couples should be granted the right to marry is, at the time of this writing, hotly debated in the U.S. Some judges have ruled that prohibitions against gay marriage violate legal protections against unequal treatment on the basis of a person's gender. As a result gay marriages are being performed in the state of Massachusetts. Legislators there and in several other states are attempting to modify their state constitutions to preclude gay marriages. This creates complications arising from the "full faith and credit" clause of the U.S. Constitution, which some legal scholars believe requires that marriages recognized in one state must be treated as valid in all states. Thus, some politicians are proposing an amendment to the U.S. Constitution, defining marriage as a union between one man and one woman.

Proponents of gay marriage believe that it is a question of fairness, while opponents believe that marriage is a special institution that should be reserved for its traditional members. Regardless of the legal outcome, the reality is that millions of American children (estimates range from one to nine million, according to the *Associated Press*)[1] are being raised by gay or lesbian parents. These children are often at the center of these controversies. Opponents of gay marriage suggest that children of gay parents are harmed, while proponents say that the harm stems strictly from the discrimination their parents face without legal recognition of their relationships as marriages. Few states permit gay couples to jointly adopt children but will permit one partner of a gay couple to do so (in the same way that a single parent can often adopt a child). A gay person may have custody of a child from a previous heterosexual relationship, or in the case of lesbian couples, one partner may bear a child with help from a sperm donor. In all these scenarios, only the legal parent (either biological or adoptive) has custody. For example, when a child is hurt, the hospital may recognize the right of only the legal parent to approve treatment. Similarly, a gay co-parent is unable to intervene at school, meaning that the child and teacher must wait until the legal parent is available. This is especially problematic when the legal parent is working and the co-parent is a full-time mom (or dad). This is more often the case than the other way around, because it is easier to obtain employer-subsidized insurance for one's legal child than it is for one's partner's child. Of course, children of gay couples can also face prejudice from teachers and other adults, as well as from their friends.

Single Parents and "Blended" Families

The high divorce rate has led to an equally high rate of remarriage. Divorce is difficult for all children, and the stress a child can experience when a parent remarries can be even more so. Stepparents, stepsiblings, half-brothers and sisters, shared custody, and the complications surrounding these relationships all have become a way of life for many Americans. Men are more likely than women to remarry, and thus many children find themselves shuttling back and forth between life with father, stepmother, and half-brothers and -sisters one week, and life with a single working mom the next week.

Managing these extended relationships is proving to be one of the most vexing social problems for millions of Americans, especially for the children. As you and your children make new friends, these "extended" family demands will add to the complexity of the social life you yourself experience. When scheduling things like carpools to work, daycare, or taking the kids to and from soccer practice, you will soon find that schedules from blended families are complicated indeed. For example, instead of being able to plan on someone every Thursday, you may find that he or she is available on alternate Thursdays only. And as you get to know the parents of your children's friends, you will likely find that you have to do everything twice for some of them — once for the father and his wife, and again for the mother and her new husband!

Americans and Their Pets

There are now more pets in the United States than there are people. According to an American Pet Products Manufacturers Association, Americans spent 32.4 billion dollars on their pets in 2003. This amount represents twice the amount from ten years earlier and is about half again as much as we spend on either toys or candy. In addition to pet food and veterinary care, most Americans buy toys for their pets. They also pay to board their pets when they go on vacation (although many take their dogs with them). In large cities, Americans hire people to walk their dogs and bathe and groom them; they drop them off early in the morning at "doggy day care" centers. Pet clothes are popular, and while most Americans think this is rather silly, it is an accepted eccentricity. Some people go so far as to think of their pets as surrogate children. According to *Doing Business with the USA* (www.diversophy.com), a full 83 percent call themselves their pet's "mom" or "dad." A survey by the American Animal Hospital Association found that 63 percent of Americans with a pet say "I love you" to their pet every day, and 44 percent would spend as much as four thousand dollars to save their pet's life. Many Americans include their pets in gift-giving holidays like Christmas and Valentine's Day, and some people even throw birthday parties for their pets!

American pets are not limited to the traditional dogs, cats, and caged birds. Rabbits, guinea pigs, caged rodents (including gerbils, hamsters, mice, and rats) are all common. Ferrets (once known as European polecats, a kind of domesticated weasel) are quite popular, as are parrots and many kinds of reptiles such as snakes and iguanas. Even pot-bellied pigs are popular!

Pets are widely believed to be good for our mental and physical health, especially for older people. In addition to pets, "companion animals" are used to assist not only the blind, but people with many other disabilities as well.

8

American Business Life

The general policy of the U.S. government has been to admit and treat foreign capital on an equal basis with domestic capital. Except in a few sensitive areas (such as communications, defense, and coastal shipping), there are few federally imposed limitations on foreign investment in the United States. However, under their own constitutions, some states have considerable power in regulating investment that falls under their jurisdiction. State laws need to be carefully understood in any business matters. Every state also has its own tax system, regulating all localities within its borders. From state to state, matters such as the availability of skilled labor, requirements for pollution control, and the like vary widely.

In 1974 the federal Committee on Foreign Investment in the United States was established to monitor the impact of direct foreign investment in the country. U.S. branches or subsidiaries (above a certain size) of foreign parent companies must register by filing quarterly reports with the U.S. Department of Commerce.

New arrivals doing business in the United States will find that U.S. economic strength has traditionally been built on the private business sector. Monopolies, cartels, and other restraints of trade are prevented by law. Some industries — for example, banking, insurance, transportation, and utilities — are government-regulated in varying degrees, but although there are many complaints about government paperwork, there is, in fact, far less federal regulation than in many other highly developed economies.

Much of the required paperwork results from close scrutiny by a wide range of government agencies over such matters as taxation, consumer protection, food and drugs, environmental controls, and equal labor opportunities. Many such protections have, in fact, been added as a result of the efforts of concerned citizens.

Labor Unions

A new arrival will find considerable differences regarding trade unions in the United States, largely because of the enormous size of the country and the diversity of American workers. There are several national unions, but most of these operate through regional or local chapters. The extent to which labor is organized at all varies a good deal, depending on both the type of industry and the region of the country. The amount of power a given union can exert also varies considerably. The most highly unionized industries are mining, construction (including all its subdivisions such as electrical work and plumbing), manufacturing, printing, airlines, and public utilities. Among the least unionized are the professions, such as medicine, law, banking, and insurance, although nurses and public school teachers are often union members. Service jobs are usually not unionized, although there are exceptions, and there is considerable debate about unionization in that sector.

Contracts between management and unions are for fixed periods of time, enforceable by law. "Wildcat," or unauthorized, strikes are rare; authorized strikes usually take place as a contract expires, almost as part of the bargaining process. Very often both labor and management know about them in advance and plan accordingly.

Labor unions have been under considerable pressure from well-organized and well-financed business organizations determined to reduce union power. In earlier years organized labor had great political power, working to elect those candidates across the country who would represent their interests in the legislative process. But business has its own election strategies and has developed strong political action committees that are now working hard to support business-oriented candidates at every level of government — national, state, and local.

Women in the Working World

As discussed in Chapter 7, the influx of women into the job market continues at a rapid pace. Most are still employed in jobs traditionally filled by women: clerical, sales, production, education, nursing, and service. Growing numbers, however, are moving into the higher-level, well-paid positions and professions once reserved almost exclusively for men. Women now outnumber men among undergraduate and graduate students, even in many professional schools such as law and medicine. Analysts expect this trend toward increased numbers of women in the workforce to continue, in no small measure because inflation and rising costs make it necessary for women to work, and also because more and more women choose to work at careers outside the home. In many families two paychecks are necessary to meet the high costs of a moderate standard of living. The poor have always struggled to make ends meet; now the middle class is also struggling.

There has been, in recent years, a push for a "living wage," meaning a wage that will support a single-worker household (assuming a small family!). This push is unlikely to have any serious long-term impact, however. The two-income household is likely to remain a necessity, or at least a perceived necessity. In addition, as Americans get married and have children later in life than in the past, both men and women are expected to work.

Job Sharing and Part-Time Work

Many middle-class, two-wage families are trading down their lifestyle so that one parent can stay at home with the children, at least on a part-time basis, whether temporarily or permanently. A relatively new trend resulting from changing values and lifestyles is the increase in part-time or job-shared work. Also, many who are old enough to retire prefer to keep active by working a few hours a day or a few days a week.

Many businesses are receptive to this change and, indeed, encourage it, because in many cases it enables them to avoid paying benefits such as pension plans and health insurance, which they must provide to full-time employees.

Rather than a deterioration of the work ethic, this interest in part-time work reflects a reordering of priorities. Adjustments can be made to accommodate education, work, family responsibilities, and leisure, although at varying levels of intensity. Furthermore, communities may benefit from the additional time that is devoted to worthwhile activities such as volunteering at a hospital or making improvements on one's home, and from the increase in the number of available jobs.

There is sense to the trend; all may benefit when the system accommodates people who need to work but do not need (or want) to do so full-time.

Attitudes toward Foreign Investments in the U. S.

Americans worry about reports of increasing numbers of foreigners gaining control of assets, including property, worth billions of dollars in the United States. "When we turn ownership of our heritage — our property and our resources — over to outside people, we are giving them political power. That is the same thing as economic power; we should recognize it as such," said one concerned businessman. Workers across the country worry about working under foreign bosses. Few realize that the amount of U.S. money invested abroad is still much higher than that of foreign money invested in the United States. Still fewer have any understanding of the extent to which foreign money is then being reinvested in the United States, nor do they understand the benefits derived from that investment.

In short, you will find Americans echoing exactly the same objections often voiced by people in other countries when foreign firms invest heavily in their economies. However, most Americans have foreign roots and many still feel the pull of old ties. As individuals, most people from abroad can expect to be welcomed, even though the notion of "foreigners" in the abstract may raise suspicion. The problems of illegal immigration have made Americans aware of those who are here with proper visas and those who are not. With resources and jobs steadily decreasing, some states, especially those that border Mexico, have made illegal immigration a political issue. On the other hand, the many Americans who are profiting from foreign investment naturally welcome the trend and, therefore, will also welcome sojourners to this country. Foreign-owned plants are welcomed when they are established in areas where additional jobs, investments, and tax revenues are needed. Real estate people are, of course, delighted. Many large-scale farmers have sold land at great profit to foreign buyers. Many states — and even many cities — are actively competing abroad for foreign investment, offering special tax exemptions and favorable financing to investors who settle in their areas. Those who come bringing business with them are not likely to perceive a mood of isolationism.

Despite the surge of patriotism since September 2001, Americans are still largely welcoming to foreign firms. Although there was a decline of foreign direct investment after 9/11, it should be noted that it was a global phenomenon, more probably a result of uncertain economies than a lack of enthusiasm. It is also true, however, that in 2002 China surpassed the U.S. as the greatest recipient of foreign investment.

Risk Takers and Experimenters

"Nothing ventured, nothing gained" is a proverb that sums up our attitude toward risk. We believe that all progress comes from being willing to take a chance. At the heart of the American economy lie thousands and thousands of small businesses, accounting for half of the private sector employment in the United States. During economic downturns, small businesses account for nearly all of the net new jobs. Working for a "startup" firm for relatively low wages (but with stock options) is still considered by many Americans to be far preferable than working for a large company with greater security but comparatively limited growth potential. This is still true, despite the "dot-com bust" of the late nineties and early twenty-first century.

According to the Bureau of Labor Statistics, half of all new businesses close within four years. This entrepreneurial spirit is perhaps the soul of American business, and government policies (for example, exempting small businesses from many requirements that affect larger businesses) ensure that this remains true. We inherited this love of risk directly from our pioneer forebears.

North Americans come from a frontier past. Many of us stem from rebel stock; we are descendants of people who braved terrible hardships in order to flee conditions at home and who took great risks to settle a new land. That same spirit has motivated wave after wave of immigrants to come to the United States, leaving one world and seeking another. The nation's frontier past and the subsequent waves of determined immigrants have forged a strong element of risk taking in the nation's character. We are always looking for the next frontier, a new challenge.

This exploratory element, coupled with what once seemed like limitless raw materials, has also made us careless. We scrap a machine, a product, or a process in favor of something new if we consider the new to be better, faster, stronger, safer. To people from countries where raw materials have always been scarce (and where conserving has necessarily been a high priority) this is often shocking. The philosophy that it is "cheaper to scrap the old and replace it with something better" frequently seems to them to be both wasteful and foolhardy.

The American view is that no one stands still. If you are not moving ahead, you are falling behind. This attitude results in a nation of people geared, to a large degree, to researching, experimenting, and exploring. Most of its adventurer, rebel, or refugee stock has come here only during the last 200 years. The country is young and full of vitality.

Time

Because most Americans place a high value on time, they resent someone else "wasting" it beyond a certain courtesy point. This view of time may be one of the causes of our lack of patience. In the American system of values, patience is not a high priority. We begin to move about restlessly if we feel time is slipping away without some return — either in terms of pleasure, work accomplishment, or rest. Those coming from lands where time is looked upon differently may find this matter of pace to be one of their most difficult adjustments in both business and daily life.

"We are slaves to nothing but the clock," it has been said. Time is treated as if it were an almost tangible entity. We *budget* it, *save* it, *waste* it, *steal* it, *kill* it, *cut* it, and *account* for it; we also *charge* for it. Time is a precious commodity. Many people have a rather acute sense of the shortness of each lifetime. Once the sands have run out of a person's hourglass, he or she cannot be replaced. We want every minute to count.

Many newcomers to the United States will miss the opening courtesies of a business call. For example, you may miss the ritual socializing that goes with a welcoming cup of tea or coffee that may be traditional in your own country. You may miss leisurely business chats in a cafe or coffeehouse.

Normally, Americans do not assess their visitors in such relaxed surroundings over prolonged small talk; nor do they take them out for dinner or a round on the golf course while they develop a sense of trust and rapport. Rapport to most of us is less important than performance. We seek out credentials of past performance rather than evaluate a business colleague through social courtesies. Since we generally assess and probe professionally rather than socially, we start talking business very quickly.

Most Americans live according to time segments laid out in engagement calendars. These calendars may be divided into intervals as short as fifteen minutes. We often give a person two or three (or more) segments of our calendar, but in the business world we almost always have other appointments following whatever we are doing. Time is therefore always ticking in our heads.

As a result, we work hard at the task of saving time. We produce a steady flow of labor-saving devices; we communicate rapidly through fax machines, phone calls, e-mail (electronic mail), and memos rather than through personal contacts, which, though pleasant, take longer. We therefore save most personal visiting for lunch, after-work hours, or for weekend social gatherings. Even at such times, we often discuss work matters.

To us the impersonality of electronic communication has little or no relation to the importance of the matter at hand. In some countries no major business is carried on without eye contact, requiring face-to-face conversation. In the United States, too, a final agreement will normally be signed in person. However, people are meeting increasingly on television or computer screens, conducting "teleconferences" to settle problems not only in this country but also — by satellite — internationally. An increasingly high percentage of normal business is being done these days by voice or electronic device.

The United States is definitely a telephone, fax, and Internet country. This is due partly to the fact that telephone service is reliable here, whereas postal service is less efficient. Furthermore, the costs of secretarial labor, printing, and stamps are all soaring. The monthly maintenance fees on telephone lines (especially for businesses) have increased substantially in recent years, but the per-call charges have actually decreased. The telephone is quick and familiar. We can do our business and get an answer in a matter of moments. Furthermore, several people can confer together without moving from their desks, even in widely scattered locations. In a big country this is important.

In today's electronic culture, nothing matches the immediacy of e-mail. Businesses and individuals are substituting e-mail for envelopes and stamps, and even the fax machine. Computer data can be transferred from one location to another with great speed and efficiency. The word *internet* is derived from *inter*connected and *net*works. Businesses and individuals who are connected to one of these telecommunications services have access to files, mail, forums, and a great deal of data.

Some new arrivals will come from cultures where it is considered impolite to work too quickly. Unless a certain amount of time is allowed to elapse, it seems in their eyes as if the task being considered is insignificant, not worthy of substantial respect. Assignments are thus perceived to be given added weight by the passage of time. In the United States, however, it is taken as a sign of competence to rapidly solve a problem or complete a job successfully. Usually, the more important a task is, the more capital, energy, and attention will be poured into it in order to "get it moving."

Letting Emotions Show

Compared with some cultures (many Asian cultures, for example), many people in the United States make little effort to hide their emotions. On the other hand, compared with some other cultures (southern Mediterranean cultures, for example), we might appear to be rather reserved. In one study of willingness to show emotions openly at work, Americans scored near the middle of the range. That being said, this is a high-pressure country, and, especially in the cities, most people live and work under a range of stresses at home and at work. Most of us understand this fact and therefore make allowances for each other fairly readily. Our feelings are not easily hurt. "Joe is pretty uptight today," we will say, or "The meeting must have gone badly," but we are not often deeply wounded by what is said in a moment of irritation. While no one likes to be the target of someone else's anger, no one loses a great deal of "face," or status, if he or she shows various degrees of emotion occasionally. Pleasure and excitement are expressed just as readily. On the whole, most of us could be described as noisy, energetic, excitable, sometimes quick-tempered, but usually open — relatively easy to read and understand. Many of us, particularly businesspeople, tell each other (and will tell you) exactly where we stand on any issue. You will find this has both good and bad aspects. Many may find this to be an area of real adjustment when first encountering the American business world.

Directness and Confrontation

Closely related to the need to get on with the job without delay is another widespread American characteristic — *directness* (sometimes also called bluntness — see Chapter 2). Again, commonly used expressions reveal our priorities:

Get down to brass tacks.

Don't beat around the bush.

Let the chips fall where they may.

Put your cards on the table.

Tell it like it is.

It is quite normal for us to jump right into a subject and say exactly what is on our minds. We often do not disguise our comments in carefully worded phrases to save a person's face or to allow for what Latinos would call *personalismo* or the Japanese would call *tatemae*. We are not likely to withdraw from a clear-cut confrontation between two issues.

Such directness often leads to an argument. Rather than avoiding opposing viewpoints, many Americans will readily express an opinion, expecting someone else to disagree with them. You will find lively discussions of issues at parties, at sports events, in the subway, on the bus, in the classroom, at the office — in short, almost anywhere. There are some who refuse to compromise. For them, a certain viewpoint is right or wrong, black or white, good or bad; there is no middle ground. Others are more flexible, willing to listen to the opposite side and perhaps even be persuaded to change their minds.

The opposite of "telling it like it is" is *indirectness*. Many people do their best to avoid confrontations. They talk around a point, leaving room for retreat or a change of view on either side, showing their sense of respect for the other person by avoiding direct denials or negatives. An American might say, "This shipment *must* go out tomorrow," and if the reply is, "It is *impossible* for it to go out tomorrow because . . . ," there will probably be a confrontation, with both parties giving reasons for their points of view, trying to win the argument. The same conversation among those who prefer indirectness or a face-saving style might go like this:

> Manager: I certainly hope this shipment can go out no later than tomorrow because . . . .
>
> Aide: I think we may have a few problems. It may be a little bit difficult, but we will try our best.

Both know from that statement that the shipment is unlikely to go out tomorrow. However, the fact is not laid on the line directly; no one will lose face whether it goes out or not; the rough spots are smoothed. Both will try to adjust accordingly; each understands the other clearly.

Those who come from cultures that operate in this manner may find American directness hard to accept until they get used to the pattern and realize that nothing is meant personally. Their feelings may be hurt from time to time as they look for grace, kindness, or dignity. Though far more courteous, indirectness is a slow approach. Americans look for speed, for facts, for clarity of meaning. The difference is a matter of priorities.

Competition and Decision Making

The predominant goal of business in the United States is financial profit, which is often referred to as "the bottom line," not family honor, personal prestige, state revenues, or any of various other goals that are primary concerns in other cultures. We spend vast sums on nationwide advertising campaigns; we compete for markets from every billboard, newspaper, and television screen. Hurried "working lunches" at one's desk, quick flights to do business in far places are part of this competitive pattern. So is the growing number of "workaholics," people who want so much to get to the top or make a corporate name for themselves that they scarcely take time out for their own families, for recreation, or for pleasure.

Contrary to the custom in many countries, decisions are made at various working levels in most American firms; they do not all get made at the top. Department, division, and section heads in the United States frequently consult with colleagues and subordinates who have relevant knowledge.

Then, depending on the type and magnitude of the decision being made, they will either make a judgment themselves or take the matter to a higher level. Even top executives normally consult one or more individuals — perhaps a board of trustees, directors, or advisers — if the matter is important, before making their own final, sometimes lonely, decision.

Negotiating

In this country negotiating is carried on in an open and direct manner at the negotiating table. It is rarely a rubber-stamp confirmation of a decision already made elsewhere, in private discussions. Americans press hard. One can assume that their eyes are firmly focused on the profit potential, whether this be long-term or short-term. Like businesspeople in most countries, they bargain. Their first monetary figure should be considered negotiable. When they lower a price, it should not be read as a sign of uncertainty or lack of trustworthiness, though it may seem so to those whose normal negotiating patterns do not involve bargaining. In the United States, compromises are the name of the negotiating game — "I will do this if you will do that."

Putting things down on paper — initial drafts — can seem threatening to people who normally do not write matters down until they are firm. Americans, however, find it imperative to get basic essentials down on paper so they can think them over and discuss, revise, and reevaluate them. No one should feel that a first draft is binding; it is not. *Nothing* is ultimately binding until it is signed by both parties, although verbal contracts or "gentlemen's agreements" as well as shared expressed perceptions are normally honored as proceedings develop.

Most foreign businesspeople who negotiate with Americans will already have had experience along these lines. If not, they should discuss American approaches and procedures with a number of people in advance. Negotiating is always a complex process. It is a sensitive area in which cultural differences, priorities, and values play a particularly significant role. This fact should be understood from the start.

Because of conflicts experienced by enterprises doing business internationally, more and more emphasis has been placed on the need for formal intercultural training. Some firms have built in this training by employing full-time trainers; others obtain the services of professional trainers as needed. The cross-cultural awareness resulting from such training has apparently made negotiating easier and has increased efficiency and, thus, profitability.

Tax Compliance and Corporate Fraud

Nobody enjoys paying taxes, wherever they live. However, where governments back massive welfare, housing, or school programs and build miles of highways, they must have money. Tax evasion in the United States is considered "fraud" and is looked upon as a serious offense. Computers check the tax returns of rich and poor alike; audits from the Internal Revenue Service are widespread. When rich tax evaders are caught, they are subject to the same penalty rates that apply to the poor. This is not true in all countries — as many readers well know. But here tax evasion is front-page scandal when a wealthy, highly placed person or corporation is found evading the tax laws. According to American law, private interests are subordinate to the public good. Since tax evasion is regarded as affecting the welfare of the entire community and nation, it is looked upon as a major offense — not worth trying!

Tax evasion isn't the only concern with corporate accounting. Some large American firms have been caught manipulating their books so they appear to be more profitable than they actually were. In so doing, the increase in their stock values more than offset any additional taxes they have had to pay. The resulting scandals, most notoriously involving the giant energy broker Enron and the telecommunications firm MCI WorldCom, have shaken the faith that many people once had in American businesses.

Life in the Office

Some office procedures may be unfamiliar, and matters of time and pace may be different. For most offices the work day normally starts at 9:00 A.M.; earlier is not uncommon, especially for managerial positions in the Western part of the country, which helps coordinate conference calls across time zones. This means nine o'clock sharp — not ten past or half past. You will find some people taking liberties with their starting times, but employers notice this even though they do not necessarily reprimand.

Employees in many nations have a philosophy that one works when the boss is present; any time he or she is not there, if there is nothing specific or pressing to do, one can relax by reading the newspaper, talking with other employees, or otherwise passing the time in a personal way. In the U.S., it is more common to think of one being paid for one's *time*. Employees are expected to find other work if their own desks are clear, to finish anything pending from previous days, or to help others with their work — but almost *never* to sit idle. The employer expects value for the salary being paid. The saying "Time is money" means exactly that. Many employers work as hard as, if not harder than, the employees, often working through the lunch hour and even taking work home at night.

Employees' lunch hours should be kept within the allotted time (unless one is officially discussing company business). Long lunchtime absences may be overlooked now and then, but not habitually. Also, although others may start getting ready to leave the office a few minutes early, new employees should be careful not to cut the day short. Work until the day officially ends at 5:00 P.M., unless you are in an office where flexible schedules are the accepted procedure. Among salaried employees, there is often intense but unspoken competition to be the hardest worker. In many companies, it is customary for employees to wait until the boss has departed before they feel they can leave. Ironically, among bosses, there is pressure to be seen as harder working than their subordinates, leading to a "stalemate" of bosses and employees each waiting for the other to leave so that they can go home!

In some places, people work on "flextime," which means staggered hours for arriving and departing. It is designed to ease congested roads and crowded commuter trains and to fit better with individuals' personal and family requirements. In 1991 over 15 percent of the workforce (approximately 12,118,000 people) were on flextime, and this number doubled in the past decade to over 25 million workers. Although originally conceived to meet the needs of mothers who work outside the home, 20 percent of workers who request flextime are women without children and, increasingly, men. Interestingly, the looser time system appears to result in greater worker productivity, higher morale, and less absenteeism.

Telecommuting — doing work from home (or from a convenient office near home) using a computer to maintain contact with the office — is becoming commonplace, although not as common as some had predicted. Still, some 32 million Americans were telecommuting by 2001, and that number is increasing. While many people miss the sociability and stimulus of the office and do not want to work out of their homes, it has benefits for both employees and employers. Many telecommuters work at home one or more days a week, and commute to work the old-fashioned way on the other days.

Hiring and Firing

People from cultures where families have close bonds are accustomed to family ties being closely connected with business. This rarely happens in the United States (except for small businesses being passed down to a son or daughter or one owned by several relatives) — and is generally distrusted. We call it "nepotism" and fear it as a corrupting influence or the taking of unfair advantage over outsiders. Nor do we develop a *patron* or permanent relationship between employer and employee. In many countries people relax once they have a job, knowing they will almost never be fired (except for a major violation of law or morality). Legal protections vary from state to state. In some states, employees cannot be unjustly fired without cause; in others, employers can terminate the employment relationship at will. Except in cases of racial, sexual, religious, or national origin (another way to express ethnicity), discrimination by employers is legal in many locations. More recently, discrimination on the basis of physical or mental disability has been outlawed, but the scope and limitations of these protections are still to be defined by the judicial system.

In any case, jobs are not permanent. Workers must do a good job, produce well, and get along with their colleagues — or they can be fired, or "let go," as it is called. Losing one's job to reorganization, outsourcing, or "down-sizing" is perhaps the most common reason for job loss. This is rarely done without warning, but it is important to be aware of the fact that in the United States one is a member of a business firm and not a family. It makes a difference.

Informality

The informality found in many offices here can prove to be a difficult adjustment for those who are accustomed to clearly defined rank in the workplace. The protocol of rank often exists here too, especially in large city banks, law firms, or major corporations. But in many establishments the atmosphere is informal and relaxed, with considerable joking, teasing, and wandering in and out of offices among all levels of employees. This may be perplexing at first for a newcomer who does not realize that, despite the informal use of first names and lots of small talk, people know very well who is in charge. The manager, the shop foreman, the "boss" does hold authority, though outward signs of this authority may not be clearly visible. To people from some countries there will be a real adjustment as they find themselves working under — or as coequals with — women. This happens more frequently in some areas of the country and in some businesses than in others, but generally women are increasingly evident in executive and managerial jobs.

Informal clothing such as sweaters, sport jackets, and casual shoes are worn in many offices, especially those outside the large cities or in certain industries, such as the software industry. In some areas even blue jeans, shorts, or open-necked shirts are common. This should not be taken for lack of respect as might be assumed in some countries. Here it has to do with local custom, or the weather, but does not relate to respect.

Social Life

Social life among employees varies tremendously from office to office. Big corporations may have singing groups, bowling or baseball teams, trips, dance or exercise classes, or other employee activities, which you can join or not as you like. Small companies usually do not.

It is quite acceptable for men or women colleagues (whether single or married) to go out together for lunch. This may be the extent to which you are invited to socialize with office friends. Although many Americans readily invite colleagues to dinner at their homes, some do not want to mix business and social life. If this is the case in your place of work, you will have to seek your friendships through other channels.

If people rush quickly out of the office in the evening without any courtesies, think nothing of it. Often they must travel long distances to get home and are hurrying to catch special trains or buses, or have other obligations such as picking up their children at school or day care by an appointed time.

Staff Meetings

Staff meetings are a regular part of most office routines. Those of all ranks are sometimes expected to contribute freely to the discussion if they have something worthwhile to add or suggest. They are not expected to make long speeches or to speak too many times in the course of a meeting. Make your point briefly and clearly, then be quiet unless asked to develop it more fully. If you have something worth saying, you probably should say it. If you are unsure, ask your supervisor in private to clarify expectations of you. People will think you have no ideas unless you express them.

Coffee Breaks

Nearly all large offices and factories have midmorning and midafternoon coffee breaks. Although fifteen minutes are allotted twice a day for relaxation and conversation, many office employees take coffee to their desks and keep on working. In small offices, the coffeepot is often on all day, and employees have coffee whenever they like, or they can make tea for themselves.

Collections

Don't be startled if someone asks you to make a contribution toward a wedding, baby, or retirement present for a fellow employee. This is often done. Everyone is likely to contribute a small amount so that a gift can be given in the name of the whole office. It is impolite to refuse, whether or not you know — or like — the particular recipient. The amount per person is usually small, and the requests are infrequent. When you leave, you will receive some recognition too!

Perquisites or "Perks"

At the upper staff levels there are often some perquisites, such as club memberships, cars, and the like; in addition, salespeople may take customers fishing or hunting, to sports events, or to theaters to attract their business. However visible, perks play far less a role in the United States than in many countries. Invisible perks include medical and life insurance, financial consulting, pensions, child-care facilities, and a variety of similar benefits.

Business Cards

Printed business cards are widely used in the United States but not as immediately or universally as they are in some countries. Do with yours whatever is comfortable, but do not be surprised if host businesspeople in the United States do not produce their cards at moments that would seem normal to you. Generally, they are exchanged in this country when two people decide they want to be in touch with each other again — not usually at the moment of meeting.

Sexual Harassment

Federal and state laws in the United States have been enacted that make sexual harassment illegal, and thus it cannot be tolerated in the workplace. If you come to the United States to work or to attend school, you should learn about company and school policy related to this issue. It is important for everyone to know what it is. This policy grew out of the principle that men and women have equal status in every facet of life and thus deserve respect from each other. Behavior that may seem jovial, such as telling jokes with sexual content or commenting on the physical attractiveness (or unattractiveness) of a coworker can be construed as harassment. So too can sincere compliments or romantic overtures, if they are unwelcome. Some companies even have prohibitions against "fraternizing," or dating, among employees. Since harassment can manifest itself in many forms, it is important for employers and employees to understand the law and their company's official policy.

Part III

Getting Here and Getting Settled

9
Getting Here

After September 11, 2001, the United States began a series of initiatives intended to enhance the security of our borders. Fierce debate continues to rage about these initiatives, with some people arguing that the government has not gone far enough and that our borders are still too porous. Others have begun to complain that at least some of these initiatives are too cumbersome and just plain unwelcoming. They argue that new policies provide more hassles than real security, and that the cost to the United States — in reduced tourism, trade, and fewer foreign students and scholars coming to the U.S. — will hurt us in ways that far exceed any real benefits. In any event, traveling to the United States has become more complicated in recent years. Changes in immigration and customs regulations may result in much longer processing times for visas, work permits, shipment of your belongings, and so on. It cannot be emphasized enough that advance planning is needed. It is imperative to understand as much of the bureaucracy as possible before you leave your country. Entering with the wrong visa type can mean months of frustrating delays and unnecessary (not to mention expensive) trips back home.

Immigration and Customs

One effect of these changes has been the reorganization of the former Immigration and Naturalization Service (INS). In the United States, permission to enter the United States is determined by two different parts of the United States government. Visas, which are stamps in passports, are granted by the Department of State at a U.S. consulate or embassy in your country. The visa is just the first step; it is simply permission to *apply for entry* at a port of entry (usually an international airport) *for a particular purpose.* The second is clearing immigration at your port of entry. The official at the airport is an employee of the Customs and Border Patrol, part of which was formerly known as the Immigration and Naturalization Service. This new agency combines the immigration inspectors at points of entry into the United States, the customs department, and the part of the Department of Agriculture that looks for illegal plant imports. Customs and Border Control is part of the new Department of Homeland Security.

One of the most significant changes in the process of coming to the U.S. is a new requirement that biometric data (primarily fingerprints) be taken on each person entering the country. Although it is to be phased in over time, it is quite likely that by the time you read this, it will be required of everyone. Even those from countries participating in the Visa Waiver Program (those coming for short stays, for tourism or business, primarily from Australia, New Zealand, Japan, and Western Europe) will be required to have a passport with biometric identifiers.

Visas

As mentioned above, visas are granted by consular officials who work in consulates or embassies outside the United States. Overworked and understaffed, they typically have to decide to grant or deny a visa application in under a minute. It is essential to be prepared for your visa interview. Rehearse your answers to the questions you might expect, such as where you plan to live while in the U.S. and how long you will be there. Given the short time the consular officers have to make a decision, they are strongly inclined to deny most applicants who hesitate with their answers. Bring with you every document related to both your proposed stay in the United States and to your ties to your own country. Most visa applicants must prove that they intend to return to their home country at the conclusion of their stay. Documents that show you own property, have close family remaining, or will be employed upon your return can be very helpful. If you are denied a visa at first, don't panic. You can usually apply again without a waiting period, although the fee has to be paid each time you apply.

Tourists and businesspeople from certain countries do not need visas *if their visit will be fewer than ninety days.* Those who come on this Visa Waiver Program *cannot,* under any circumstances, extend their stay or change the purpose of their visit. It is essential to take the time to obtain the correct type of visa before you leave home. Each visa type has its own limitations and benefits, so seeking advice from a qualified immigration attorney is prudent. The American Immigration Lawyers Association (www.aila.org) can help you find one.

Immigration

Your entry into the U.S. may be granted or denied (or delayed) by the Customs and Border Patrol officer, called an *inspector.* She or he will admit you for a period of time consistent with the type of visa you have in your passport. If you were not fingerprinted when you obtained a visa, it is likely that you will be fingerprinted at this point. Most people who know others who have traveled to the U.S. have heard at least one horror story about being ill-treated by an immigration official. Sadly, there are indeed people who are unpleasant or rude, even threatening. But rarely do we hear about the millions — literally millions — of entries that go off smoothly and end with a cheerful "Enjoy your visit."

It is important to remember that no immigration inspector wants to be the one who lets a person with terrorist plans into the United States. The officers are understandably cautious and will expect you to be able to prove any claims you make. If you have letters from colleagues or friends you are visiting, bring them. If you are planning to study in the U.S., have your letters of admission and I-20 form or other documents ready.

Particularly if you are from countries that the U.S. government believes have links to terrorists or, sadly, from any Middle Eastern country, be especially ready for some questioning about your plans during your stay in the U.S. What these officers are trained to do is look for inconsistencies in your answers, or for body language that indicates someone is lying. If you are relaxed and answer honestly, even if you don't know an answer, you will not likely be singled out for more attention. Remember to look the inspector in the eye; Americans in general, and immigration inspectors specifically, distrust anyone who won't make eye contact at least some of the time. On the other hand, don't stare either.

Customs

The Customs Agency is concerned with what you are bringing into the U.S. They make sure that what you bring is permissible and that duty, or import tax, is collected if it is due. Personal property is usually not subject to duty, but if you bring, for example, one hundred compact discs of your favorite artist to give as gifts, you might appear to be an importer rather than a student.

You may be asking yourself, "What *can* I bring into the United States without paying duty?" "Can I bring gifts?" "Must I declare *everything*?" "Is there anything that I may not bring?"

You should obtain from the nearest U.S. consulate a copy of the pamphlet *Customs Hints for Visitors (Nonresidents)*, which gives full answers to all such questions. Below are *summaries* of the regulations.

Not Allowed

Some items that may *not* be brought into the United States without special permits are listed below.

1. *Medications.* If you must bring in a special prescription, be *sure* to get a permit in advance. Inquire at a U.S. consulate for details.

2. *Plants.* No fruits, vegetables, plants, seeds, cuttings, or plant products may be imported without writing ahead for permission. The reason for this regulation is that the United States is attempting to prevent insects or plant diseases from being brought into the country. Contact the U.S. Department of Agriculture (www.aphis.usda.gov/ppq/).

3. *Meats and hides.* To avoid importing animal diseases, permission is needed to bring in meats (including dried fish, sausages, salamis, etc.) and untanned furs or hides. If you wish to bring any of these to the United States, write to

   Animal Health Division
   U.S. Agricultural Research Service
   Hyattsville, MD 20782
   www.usda.gov/

4. *Goods from certain countries.* One cannot import goods of any kind originating in certain countries. Inquiries should be made to

> Foreign Assets Control
> Department of the Treasury
> Washington, DC 20220
> www.ustreas.gov/offices/eotffc/ofac/

5. *Gold.* There are tight restrictions regarding gold, gold coins, gold-coin jewelry, or medals.

6. *Firearms and ammunition.* Guns and ammunition are regulated by the Alcohol, Firearms and Tobacco Bureau (www.atf.gov/firearms/feib/). No ammunition, pistols, or revolvers may be shipped in the U.S. mail.

If you have questions on customs regulations that cannot be answered by your nearest U.S. embassy or consulate, write

> Customs and Border Patrol
> Department of Homeland Security
> Washington, DC 20226
> www.customs.gov/

Pets

Cats, dogs, birds, and so on, must meet certain requirements before they may enter. Ask at the nearest U.S. consulate for the booklet *So You Want to Import a Pet,* or write

> Centers for Disease Control
> Division of Quarantine, M.S. E03
> Atlanta, GA 30333
> (404) 639-8107
> www.cdc.gov/ncidod/dq/animal.htm

Dependents

If you are coming as a student, or to work for a particular employer who has filed a petition on your behalf, you can also bring your spouse and unmarried children under 21 years of age. They will need their own passports and visas. They may study in the primary and secondary schools (see Chapter 19) in the United States, but unless you are working for your own government or an international government agency (and have the appropriate nonimmigrant status), your dependents may not be employed in the U.S. If your spouse or child wishes to attend college, he or she will need to obtain a student status. The foreign student adviser at the college or university your student will attend can help.

If you have a non-spousal partner (a domestic partner who is not your husband or wife) or if you have domestic servants who have been in your employ for at least one year, they can apply for a special version of the tourist (B-2) or business (B1) visa. This will make it easier for them to renew their stays in the United States.

Shipping Your Belongings

If you are renting a furnished apartment or house, moving is a relatively simple matter. You move exactly as you would for a stay in a hotel, although you might bring a few extra items.

If you are moving all your household goods to this country, you or your company will probably have arranged the transfer through a specialist. Large national and international movers have experienced packers and good equipment. You should inventory all your belongings carefully, making separate lists of those items that are going into storage, those being shipped to your new home, and those going to be cared for in some other way.

Inventories should be reasonably detailed, but you can group together and record the number of boxes of kitchen items, children's clothing, desk contents, and so forth. You do not have to itemize down to the last spoon.

Before any packers or movers come, you should sort out your belongings into separate categories as much as you can. Mark storage goods and those to be shipped with different-colored tags or stickers to avoid confusion or errors. You must also carefully supervise the movers as they work.

As the boxes are being packed for your new destination, mark each completed carton clearly in large letters on the outside as books, children's toys, kitchen supplies, and so on. This will help both the movers and you when you finally get into your new home.

When you discover how expensive it is to ship household goods, you will probably agree that it often makes better sense to buy basic equipment, such as dishes, sheets, towels, and saucepans, here rather than to ship your own — unless, of course, your company is assuming all shipping costs.

Furthermore, you may want to think carefully about bringing any pieces of furniture or cherished items, such as a delicate clock, an antique desk, your favorite chair. The best rule to follow is this: if the item were lost or broken, how would you feel? Picture the crate being lifted by a ship's crane and then dropped into the ship's hold or sitting on a dock during a heavy rain. Probably neither of these things will happen, because most goods today are packed well, but think about the possibility of such hazards. You may decide to leave your most valued possessions at home.

What will the climate be like in the part of the United States to which you are going? If you will be in sunny California, hot Arizona, or moist Florida, you should consider leaving heavy rugs, big upholstered chairs, velvet draperies, and the like at home. In hot areas it is practical to use rattan, glass, or wicker and to use louvers or shutters rather than draperies at the windows.

Clothes You Will Need

Winter temperatures throughout much of the country range from 0°F (or below) to about 65°F (-20°C to 18°C). You should also be prepared for a good deal of wind. For outdoor wear, insulated coats or down parkas with hoods, warm mittens or gloves, and a hat and scarf are essential in many places in the North. Many people do not realize that 75 percent of heat loss is through radiation from the head; a warm hat (one that covers the ears) is one of the best ways to brave the cold. There is often snow, but in most cities it is quickly cleared, especially in the northernmost part of the country where cities are well equipped with sand, salt, and snowplows. In southern areas, the winter climate is much warmer.

Indoors, in winter, buildings are likely to be kept somewhere around 65°–68° (18°–20° Celsius) or higher — much warmer than in Europe. You will need lightweight wool for winter, with additional sweaters, jackets, coats, or ponchos to put on or take off easily as you move from outdoors to indoors. Those who come from hot climates will perhaps feel the cold very much at first and should be prepared with layers, such as extra scarves or sweaters, and warm underwear. You will also need a light jacket during the four in-between months of spring and autumn (April-May and September-October). The combination type with removable zip-out lining is especially useful. A raincoat and umbrella are essential almost everywhere in the U.S., except for the driest areas of the Southwest.

Summer in much of the U.S. is *hot*. Temperatures in the 90s (low to mid 30s Celsius) are not uncommon even in areas known for their winter cold, such as Minnesota. In the Midwest and the Southeast, summertime humidity makes the warm temperatures even more uncomfortable. In the Southwest, temperatures can soar to 115 degrees Fahrenheit (46 degrees Celsius). Although people like to say "But it's a dry heat" (meaning that lower humidity makes it less uncomfortable), newcomers usually take some time to adjust to these extremes. Needless to say, central air conditioning is considered a near-necessity in these areas.

Specific research on the areas you will be visiting or living that take into account the time of year of your visit will help assure your comfort. Remember too that the prevalence of discount stores means that outfitting yourself and your family after you arrive need not be an unduly expensive proposition.

Americans in general like bright colors, and dress is informal, even in the cities. Few women wear hats, for example, except during cold, windy weather or for very dressy occasions such as weddings. Dark business suits for men and cocktail dresses for women suffice at most evening functions. People rarely wear formal attire (tuxedos and long evening dresses) for the theater except on opening nights of professional productions.

Children and teenagers dress very casually except for special occasions when they are dressed in party clothes. In many parochial schools and a small number of other private schools, uniforms are required (indeed, a few public schools are experimenting with required uniforms). Some schools still require jackets and ties for boys (or just ties). In general, though, boys and girls wear a variety of sturdy and informal clothes to school, often jeans and T-shirts, sweatshirts, or sweaters. During the summer months children and teenagers often wear shorts and T-shirts. The trend for teenagers is increasingly individualistic — even bizarre. Dress-up occasions can be quite competitive, ranging anywhere from "doing your own thing" to formal dresses and suits, depending on the geography and on personal taste. The cost of outfitting a teenager for a prom (a kind of formal school dance) can be quite a shock for some newcomers.

10
Money and Banking

You should have a minimum of one to two hundred dollars in American currency (in small bills) upon arrival at a U.S. airport, for tips to porters and for transportation into the city. There are money exchanges in all international airports, but it is a bother to stop at the moment of arrival when you also have to cope with immigration, customs, luggage, crowds, and fatigue. It is better to convert an adequate supply of money before departing. Taxi fares are rising rapidly in this country, and airports are generally several miles outside the city. Airport buses are much less expensive and are recommended unless you have a large number of people in your group or considerable luggage. A bus will take you to a central point in the city from which you can hire a cab to your final destination at far lower cost. Ask about them at the information desk at the airport. Many large hotels provide their own transportation (shuttle) to and from the airport; in some cases hotel guests may ride free of charge, and others may ride for a reasonable fee. A few cities have light rail service to their major airports.

Coins and Bills

American money can be quite confusing — one observer has concluded that our coinage was designed deliberately to confuse foreigners! After many years of circulation, the "greenback" look of U.S. currency is changing. The ten-, twenty-, and fifty-dollar bills have been updated in recent years with larger type, more colors, and greater security features. U.S coins, none of which has a numerical representation of their value, are as follows: 1 cent (penny), 5 cents (nickel), 10 cents (dime), 25 cents (quarter), and occasionally one-dollar coins. You may occasionally find a fifty-cent coin (half dollar), but there are very few still in circulation. All coins are silver-colored except for the penny, which is copper-colored, and the Sacagawea dollar, which is a gold color. You may also occasionally find a Susan B. Anthony dollar coin, which is slightly larger than a quarter, with smooth edges. Although the coins can be confusing, they are still considerably easier to understand than are our weights and measures!

You often need to keep considerable change on hand, especially in cities, where exact change for buses is often required. Bus drivers are not allowed to make change in many cities. You may have to buy tokens or fare cards for bus travel. Ask where to do this, as it varies by city. Sales tax requires small coins, although stores will make change if needed. One confusing practice is that the list price of most items almost never includes the sales tax, which varies from state to state and even from city to city. Certain items in some localities are not taxed — food taken out, for example, or clothing up to a certain amount. Sales tax rates vary from 0 percent in some places to 8 percent or more in others!

Bills, or paper money, are all similar in color and size. You will have to look carefully to be sure you are using a $1 bill and not a $10 bill, for example. Bills that you are likely to use come in the following denominations: $1, $5, $10, $20, $50, and $100. The $50 and $100 bills are not carried by many people. You would be wise to carry only small-value bills ($20 bills or lower) with you. Taxi drivers, subway attendants, and some store clerks will not change anything larger than a twenty-dollar bill; most supermarkets and large department stores will, however.

It is a good idea to get a selection of American coins and bills from your bank before leaving home and practice with them so that you can recognize them easily. If you do this with children, too, they can also become comfortable with the currency before they even arrive.

There is no limit to the dollars you may bring into or take out of the United States; however, large cash sums must be declared at customs; in addition, your own country may restrict the amount you are allowed to take with you. You will need to check on that before leaving home.

Banks

You may find that banks in the United States operate quite differently from banks in your country. Before you open a checking or savings account, ask a bank officer about the various checking and savings plans and the rules and regulations regarding such features as free checking, required balances, purchasing checks, making deposits, ATM (automated teller machine) cards, and overdrafts. The banking business has become very competitive, so you may find a large, and sometimes confusing, array of accounts available. The ones described here are available in most banks but may be listed under different names.

Some checking accounts require a specific balance (usually between $500 and $2,500), called a "minimum daily balance," in the bank at all times, but there is no charge for each check issued and no monthly service fee if the balance does not drop below the minimum daily balance. Other accounts, called by various names at different banks, do not require as large a balance, but there is a charge for each check and sometimes a monthly service charge as well. There are also special accounts for larger balances.

Banks charge service fees for falling below the required minimum and penalties for "bounced" checks (checks not covered by sufficient funds). Most banks allow you to combine a savings and checking account — and earn interest on the money that would usually be in the checking account. These are worth investigating; you should compare what is offered by different banks and try to choose one that offers the services you want and is convenient for you to visit. Because of changes in reporting requirements designed to track foreign source money, some banks are requiring that customers obtain a tax payer identification number (TIN) *before* they can open an account. This can be obtained through the local office of the Internal Revenue Service. If you will be employed in the United States, you will need to obtain a Social Security number, which also serves as a taxpayer identification number. This is obtained through a separate Social Security Administration office and will require proof of your employment authorization in addition to your passport and possibly proof of your U.S. address.

Taking Care with Cash and Valuables

However much money you keep in your home or in your wallet or purse, be extremely careful with it. Never leave a wallet or purse on a desk in your office or on a store counter *for even a moment,* and don't leave your purse in a supermarket basket. At home keep it out of sight and away from the entrance, and do not carry excess cash when you go out. Regretfully, purse snatching and pocket picking are quite common in metropolitan areas in the United States, as they are in other parts of the world. In today's world of electronic finance, "identity theft" (in which someone is able to use your personal information to convince others that she or he is really you, often by obtaining your credit card, bank account number, social security number, and other personal information) is a growing and serious threat. This is best avoided by keeping your identification and financial information secure from others and shredding, rather than discarding, any documents that contain such information.

If you have jewelry or other valuables (passports, wills, stock certificates, mortgage or insurance papers, leases, etc.), you may want to rent a safe deposit box at a nearby bank. This will cost from $15 to $250 per year, depending on the size of the box and the area of the country. You can get your valuables out any time during banking hours, and these irreplaceable items will be safe and protected in bank vaults. If you are staying in a hotel, have the desk clerk put jewelry and other items into the hotel safe. *Do not leave valuables in your hotel room,* even in a suitcase. Many hotels offer electronic safes in the rooms. Insure expensive or irreplaceable jewelry, furs, cameras, watches, or other items that can easily be stolen. It is worth the cost and the extra time to secure your valuables.

Sending Money Abroad

There are several ways to send money to someone in another country. If time is important, you may make arrangements at your bank by asking them to send a "wire transfer" to a bank in another country. If there is no urgency, some banks will make less expensive transfers by letters to foreign banks. If you want the bank to notify the receiver of the funds, be sure to tell them that person's address. In order to receive transferred funds, the person will have to present himself or herself at the overseas bank with proper identification.

Money can also be sent abroad through the U.S. Postal Service (see Chapter 14).

Charge Accounts and Credit Cards

The United States is becoming more and more a cashless society. People are making purchases by check, charge account, bank (debit) card, or credit card rather than carrying much money in their pockets or purses.

Most people receive monthly statements of bills and then send payment by check for charges such as department store purchases, telephone, electricity, gas, newspaper delivery, and similar household expenses. Increasingly, however, people are paying their bills through the Internet using a home computer and their bank's secure website. Many use credit cards to pay for gasoline and service station expenses and for restaurant, hotel, and travel costs. In most supermarkets a variety of payment options are available: cash, personal check, credit card, or debit card.

Many people, however, prefer not to accumulate monthly bills. They work out a combination, paying some bills in cash and charging others. This is a matter of personal choice. If you use credit cards, be sure to pay promptly; the interest charged for late payments can be high, and your credit rating can be adversely affected if you do not pay your bills by the deadline stated on the bill.

Many credit card companies charge a yearly fee and interest rates that vary from one company to the next. It is important to check the amount of the interest rate as well as the amount of the yearly fee, then select a card that will cost you the least. Competition among credit card banks and companies is tremendous. Take your time in choosing a card, and read the information provided very carefully. Some companies advertise that they charge no yearly fees and some seem to be offering low interest rates on the amount carried over on the card, but buyer beware! Read the small print; most of these great deals are not deals at all. That low interest rate may last only a month or two, then jump to one far above the market rate. The most common credit cards are Visa, MasterCard, American Express, and Discover. They can be used at most stores, restaurants, hotels, and gas stations. Some stores, however, do not accept American Express. When you receive your credit card, be sure to sign the back of it in the space provided.

Most department stores offer charge accounts; they will ask for bank and other credit references. Approval of new accounts can take from a few minutes to a few weeks. When your application is approved, you will be sent a credit card (sometimes called a "charge card") that can be used *only in that particular department store.* Charge cards greatly speed up the buying process. In addition, you can return goods and obtain a credit on your account (you will generally not get a cash refund).

There are disadvantages to having a credit or charge card. If you lose it and someone picks it up, or if someone steals your wallet, he or she can run up heavy charges on your account. If this happens to you, call the store or credit card service *immediately* and report the loss. Then *write them at once* and tell them again the day and time you phoned in to report the loss. Keep a copy of the letter. You will not be liable for any charges made on the card *after the time you first reported it.* Some people carry their credit cards only when they go shopping; others carry them whenever they go out, but whatever you do, always be on guard for possible purse snatchers or pickpockets. Visa and MasterCard do not generally hold a theft victim responsible for more than a set amount.

ATMs (Automated Teller Machines) are fast replacing bank services for withdrawing and, in some cases, even depositing money. When using an ATM, do so from a car if possible — for safety reasons. When on foot, use normal safety precautions and be sure that no one sees you enter your PIN (personal identification number). Also, ATMs usually charge a transaction fee unless your bank account is with the same bank that owns the ATM.

Tipping

Some people from other countries — and also some in the United States — are opposed to tipping, considering it undemocratic and demeaning. Furthermore, it is illogical — waiters, porters, and hairdressers are tipped, while airline attendants, store clerks, and insurance agents are not. Many feel that people should receive an adequate salary rather than tips.

However you feel about this, the fact is that in the United States many people do depend to a large extent on tips for their livelihood. In some fields of work, wages are simply not adequate. The theory is that by compensating people through tips rather than on a straight salary, you encourage good service. Although that is debatable, the system prevails.

You do not *have* to tip. If you are dissatisfied with service, you can show it by reducing or withholding a tip. But generally speaking, tipping is expected in the United States. It is a way of saying thank you to people who provide services for you. One exception to this is in a restaurant when your party is a large one. Very often a flat 15 percent gratuity is added to your bill. Check carefully in order to avoid tipping twice.

People You Tip in the United States

Waiters, taxi drivers, porters, doormen, hat-and-coat-check attendants, and delivery people should all be tipped. You also tip for personal services from barbers, shoe shiners, hair stylists (or beauticians), and so on. Parking lot attendants should be tipped only if they have parked your car or brought it for you.

Unfortunately, many employers of these workers underpay, considering tips to be part of the wages. If you do not tip, therefore, you are depriving the worker of needed income.

People You Do Not Tip

1. *Customs officials or other government employees, such as police officers or firefighters.* This is considered bribery.

2. *Postal employees and other commercial delivery people.* Although mail deliverers are not tipped, people often give them a gift around the winter holidays of five to ten dollars. The same goes for package delivery service drivers (such as United Parcel Service and Federal Express if you receive regular packages from them), as well as newspaper deliverers.

3. *Airline flight attendants or ticket agents.*

4. *Room clerks or people at hotel desks* (unlike the European concierge system).

5. *Bus drivers.* If, however, they also serve as guides on guided tours, then give them a few dollars and thank them as you leave.

6. *Store clerks.*

7. *Gas station attendants.*

8   *Elevator operators, receptionists, or telephone operators.*

9. *Employees in private clubs.*

10 *Theater or movie ushers.*

Normal Tips

Tipping customs and amounts vary considerably from one part of the United States to another, as well as from small towns to large cities. When you are settled in your area, you should ask about this locally.

To put newcomers at ease during their initial few days, the following guidelines are offered.

1. *Porters.* A dollar or two per bag is customary. Some people tip more if the bags are heavy and difficult to handle.

2. *Taxi drivers.* The driver will expect 15 to 20 percent. If there are several of you, or if you have a lot of luggage, give at least 20 percent. In some cities there is an extra charge for each passenger. Such variations are posted in the cab.

3. *Waiters.* Give at least 15 to 20 percent to the waiter. A service charge is generally not included in the bill. Give the waiter more if you are particularly satisfied with the service, have asked for extras, had a large group, or requested help in understanding the menu or in serving young children; in other words, if you have received more than normal service. If you are part of a group of six or more, a 15 percent gratuity is generally added to your bill. As in other countries, tips are naturally higher in finer restaurants. In such a place your tip for the waiter should not be less than 20 percent. If you order wine, the wine steward may expect a tip as well as the waiter. In a low-priced diner or cafe, the tip is about 10 percent, or at least a dollar per person or a quarter under your plate for just a cup of coffee or tea. If you order room service in a hotel, 15 to 20 percent of the bill is proper.

4. *Doormen.* For normal daily services, you do not tip except when they call a taxi for you. Then give them a couple of dollars. If they help with a great deal of luggage at any time, give them three to five dollars, depending on the amount of trouble taken. Most people give the doormen of their apartment houses occasional tips — ranging from one to five dollars — for any extra services they may perform, for special occasions, or for a good many small services done over a considerable

length of time (that have gone untipped). This is not required, but it helps to keep service friendly and helpful.

5. *Personal services.* It is hard to give a rule of thumb as to how much to tip barbers, hairdressers, delivery people, parking lot attendants, the maid who looks after your hotel room, and other people who serve you. Rates vary, depending on the part of the country, how much service they have given, and other factors. The best advice is to ask locally, though if you ask four or five people in your office, at a party, or in your neighborhood about tipping, you will undoubtedly receive varied answers. If you cannot find anyone to ask easily, you can say directly to the person involved, "I would like to give you something extra for your service but I am a stranger here. What is the normal tip?" Almost surely you will get a big smile and an honest answer.

6. *The holidays.* The winter holidays are special — and expensive. Here are some suggestions. If you live in an apartment house where there are doormen, give each one of them a gift of ten dollars or more during the holidays. The amount will vary, depending on how long you have been living there, the size of your family, and how many other tips you have given throughout the year. Also, the superintendent of your apartment house should receive a gift of twenty dollars or more. If there are other service people such as trash collectors, porters, or telephone operators, you may also want to give them five dollars or so. Holiday tips are also sometimes given to the tradespeople one sees regularly — the laundry attendant, newspaper deliverer, parking lot attendant, hairdresser, or barber. These tips are flexible, depending on how often they have served you and on your financial situation. But if you feel friendly toward them, three to five dollars in a holiday card would be much appreciated by any of these people who have worked for you throughout the year.

11
Medical Care

When people move to a new, unfamiliar country, they are often quite concerned about what might happen if they get sick. This is an understandable fear because medical practices and the customs that surround illness differ, sometimes dramatically, from culture to culture. Even if the medical care you receive is excellent, as it usually is in this country, there is still discomfort because it is not what you are accustomed to, and because you may be far from people who would normally assist and comfort you. The information below is intended to help you understand the practice of medicine in the United States so that you can obtain care with as little apprehension as possible.

Before You Leave Home

The first step in obtaining medical care in a new country is to bring your family's health records with you, if possible. This provides your new physician with a complete history of past medical experience and may help you save on expensive tests or background studies. Also, have all necessary dental work done before you leave home; costs for dental care in the States are nearly as high as those for medical care, and insurance rarely covers all procedures.

If you wear eyeglasses or contact lenses, have an extra pair with you and be sure to bring a copy of your prescription. If you are on regular medication, it is a good idea to bring a copy of the prescription and information from your physician at home about the condition for which the medication is required.

Obtaining Medical Care

For general medical care, most people's primary doctor is a family practice specialist — someone who will provide routine care for all members of the family and who can refer you to other kinds of specialists when necessary. There are two kinds of specialists who are often contacted immediately — a pediatrician if there is a young child in the family and a gynecologist for adolescent girls and women. Many general practitioners, however, are qualified and experienced in treating children and gynecological matters.

There are numerous medical groups that give patients access to a number of doctors rather than one. They emphasize family practice — taking care of all the medical needs of family members in one place and providing service at all times with one or another of the group members available on call. Many of these groups are referred to as health maintenance organizations, or HMOs. Some are attached to hospitals, but most are independent, and the physicians have privileges at local hospitals. Most HMOs have listings of doctors in your area who are members, and a few HMOs combine health insurance and health care into one organization.

How do you go about finding a reliable doctor? Physicians are listed in the classified telephone directory (often called the Yellow Pages), and many even advertise their services, but people usually find doctors by asking friends and acquaintances about their experiences with medical care. There are a variety of ways to search. Your company may advise you. Often there is a company doctor or an arrangement with a medical group, which is a great help. Perhaps you can ask your neighbors, or the person from whom you rent your apartment, or the head of your child's school. The officer at the bank or someone at your church, mosque, or synagogue may also give you advice. Your own consulate may have a list of doctors who speak your language.

Don't necessarily accept the first physician suggested. People have different needs. Most physicians are very well trained in the United States, so you rarely have to worry about technical competence. Probably the most important consideration, and one you can judge easily, is personality. You will want to find someone who is easy to talk with and in whom you have confidence. You may also want to inquire about costs if that is important to you.

If it is difficult to obtain a personal recommendation from someone you know, call the County Medical Society or the Physician Referral Service in your area. These offices can either provide a list of physicians or tell you where you can get this information. You can also call the administrator's office at the nearest hospital and ask for the names and office addresses of doctors with privileges at their hospital. This way you will find well-trained doctors with nearby hospital affiliations. Neither the hospital nor the County Medical Society will recommend one doctor; they will always provide several names. When you have been given the names and telephone numbers of several doctors, make an appointment with one of them. Take your family's health records and ask about fees, hospital connections, and anything else you want to know. If the doctor's experience, medical training, and personality seem right to you, you will probably want to become a regular patient and return whenever necessary. If not, you may want to look for another doctor.

Many doctors have so many regular patients that they will not accept new ones. Simply keep trying until you find one who is able to accommodate you as a patient. Don't feel shy about discussing fees when you first make these contacts. They can vary, and it is better to know in advance the approximate fees any given physician is likely to charge. Medical care is extremely expensive in the United States, and it is important to know what costs to expect.

Medical Emergencies

In most of the country the emergency number for ambulance, police, or fire is 9-1-1, but it is wise to check this locally, especially if you are far from large cities. If you do not know the emergency number, just dial "0" for the operator and tell him or her about your situation, but *do not forget to give your address and telephone number.* If you hang up without giving this critical information, you will have wasted precious moments while the operator tries to trace the call. If you can, go directly to the emergency room of the nearest hospital. Emergency rooms are set up to deal with serious accidents and acute illnesses (such as a heart attack). It is a good idea to find out where this facility is located before you need it. They are equipped to respond quickly to life-threatening situations. However, calling 9-1-1 and requesting an ambulance may be the most prudent course.

Urgent Care

If you have an urgent medical concern that does not qualify as an emergency, the first step is to call your doctor. If you do not have a doctor — or if he or she is unavailable — go to the emergency room of the nearest hospital. Less serious illnesses and accidents, although they may occur without warning, are treated by family physicians and in walk-in clinics. Some hospitals also have an "express care" or "urgent care" service, separate from their emergency services. There are even urgent care or walk-in clinics, separate from hospitals, that may provide quicker treatment of many serious (but not life-threatening) medical conditions such as broken limbs or fevers. These tend to be less expensive than the emergency room and you will not likely have to wait too long, unlike an emergency room where more serious injuries are treated before minor ones.

Although health care is expensive in the United States, it is good and in most cases very thorough. People are referred to hospitals more often here than in many other countries. If this happens to you, be sure you understand from the doctor exactly what the reason is before you become worried. It often means only that the doctor wants to make use of special facilities for tests, X-rays, or treatment procedures, or wants to have you observed at frequent intervals over a period of days by a trained staff. It does not necessarily mean that the doctor thinks you are seriously ill.

Health Insurance

Because medical costs are high, insurance is necessary. There are many excellent free public facilities for the poor, but they are so crowded and the waiting time so long that most people who can afford to use private doctors do so. More important, as a non-American (that is, until you have obtained permanent residence), you are not permitted to take advantage of publicly funded medical care. You will not be turned away, but there may be consequences later with your immigration status. As of yet, there is no national system of health care coverage (except for Medicare, which covers persons sixty-five years of age and over), but the issue is hotly debated.

At the present time, the great majority of American people subscribe to private insurance programs, which help to pay for hospital and doctor bills. You should join such a program also. If you work for an American company, there is quite likely a group insurance plan to which you and your family will automatically belong, but you should find out about this in detail. Payments for such plans are usually partially paid by the employer; your contribution is made through automatic payroll deductions. Find out exactly what the coverage includes, because this varies from one plan to another. Also, check the deductible (the amount you must pay before the insurance covers the cost). Many insurance programs require a "copay," which is a fixed amount you pay for each medical treatment. While these are usually modest, they can add up to a significant amount for those who have chronic conditions requiring frequent visits to a doctor.

If you are working for an organization that does not have group insurance, you should purchase private health insurance for yourself and your family. One bad accident or serious illness could cost you a great deal of money. Most insurance plans are open to international personnel after they have lived in the United States for six months; some will cover them earlier than that. Ask at your company about a good insurance adviser or ask your doctor. This should be done immediately after arrival in this country.

Foreign students enrolled in U.S. colleges and universities are usually required, either by their institution or by the state it is located in, to have medical insurance (by federal regulation, J-1 students and scholars *must* have insurance). They also pay their college infirmary fee, which entitles them to receive full infirmary care whenever they need it. They can also purchase additional low-cost accident insurance, which is recommended and often required. The university or college catalogue will give details, and the foreign student adviser will inform new students about the insurance plan recommended by the school. Dependent family members are often *not* eligible for infirmary care and should be covered with outside health insurance.

Medical insurance *almost never covers all expenses.* Read the policy carefully and have someone explain it to you in detail. Coverage varies widely from one policy to another. Some policies include medications and basic dental care, but few cover eyeglasses. You can have these specialties added, but the cost rises sharply with each one. Be sure to think over carefully exactly what you need, balancing the cost of the policy against those services you can afford. Eyeglasses generally cost between 50 and 200 dollars, more if you do not have your written prescription from an eye doctor.

Before selecting a health insurance agent, it is a good idea to obtain advice from a colleague or friend. Most agents are reliable, but some are not; you will need help in selecting a reputable firm.

Be prepared to present your insurance card before receiving services at a hospital. If you have no insurance, be prepared to arrange for payment of all hospital bills before taking the patient home. Your corporation or your insurance may cover such matters for you; otherwise, the hospital may demand full payment — even if this requires your taking out a loan to cover it. It is advisable to talk to your employer, your doctor, or your insurance agent about this so you will know your own situation before an emergency arises. Occasionally, hospitals will agree to have payments spread over a period of time.

12
Safety and Emergencies

E veryone knows that cities around the world are full of problems and are sometimes dangerous; however, you need not miss the many advantages cities offer if you take precautions and use common sense. Then the chances of having a misfortune — while not totally removed — are very much diminished.

Safety on the Streets

When you walk after dark, keep to the more heavily traveled and well-lit streets. If you have to go through dangerous areas, go by bus or taxi. Try to board your bus in a populated area rather than at a bus stop in a deserted locality.

Avoid parks after dark; if you are passing one, walk on the opposite side of the street. People with bad intent often loiter in dark places. They like the edges of parks because they can make a quick escape. They also like doorways and alleys. If you feel apprehensive, walk on the curb side of the sidewalk.

If you have to wait in a train or bus terminal at night, do so in the main waiting room, where it is light and people are passing, or else choose a place in sight of a guard or police officer. Avoid subway travel in the late evening when stations are likely to be fairly deserted.

Most — but not all — crime in the United States takes place in dark, rather predictable places where there are few people about. Reasonable precautions such as the above will markedly reduce your chance of trouble. Find out about neighborhoods or areas of the city to avoid after dark (or at any time).

Safety and Unescorted Women

Women who are alone are far more free here than in many parts of the world; one sees unescorted women almost anywhere. Unfortunately, however, crime is widespread here and certain precautions are necessary.

A woman can feel safe in planes, buses, and trains (day or night). It is safe for a woman to drive long distances alone. Service station attendants and hotel and motel personnel will give friendly help; if there is trouble with the car along the way, a single woman will nearly always get help from passersby (although here, too, caution should be exercised) or the highway patrol. If your car does break down, you should try to pull as far off the road on the right side as possible. Turn on the emergency flashers and raise the hood, then wait with the car for help to arrive. In most locations, even on deserted stretches of road, a highway patrol car will arrive before too long. But if a woman (or a man, for that matter) is driving alone in a city, it is wise to keep the car doors locked and valuables out of sight. These two simple habits can prevent someone from jumping quickly into the car at a stoplight or grabbing something through an open window.

Cities become less safe after dark. Stay on well-populated and well-lit streets; take taxis after about 9:00 P.M. Hold your purse carefully, don't let shoulder bags hang loosely, and don't wear valuable jewelry until you reach your destination. With the high price of gold and gems, jewelry is a hot item among thieves.

It is best to ask locally which streets (and areas) are safe and which are not, although the responses often reveal as much information about your informant's prejudices as about the safety realities. Remember that looks can be deceiving; some dark areas can be safe; well-lit ones may be dangerous at quiet times (such as Wall Street after the business world goes home). Visitors to the United States should be particularly careful about safety. Until you have been here for a while, you won't know how to judge whether a situation, a person, or a place is dangerous because you won't know how to "read" the clues.

Security at Home

As humorist Garrison Keillor once observed, there are still small towns in the U.S. where some people not only refuse to lock their doors, they forget where they put their keys years ago! Nevertheless, locks only work if you use them. Never leave the door to your house, hotel, or apartment unlocked; be careful not to leave a key in the door by mistake, even for a short time. Also, don't leave your door open, ajar, or unlocked, even if you are just going out to empty the trash or talk with a neighbor. It is a good precaution to use the inside chain on the door, especially at night. Most hotels, apartments, and homes are now equipped with dead-bolt locks in addition to the regular locks on the doorknobs.

Most city apartments have peepholes through which you can see who is at your door before you open it. Others have TV systems in the front lobby or some voice identification arrangement. Use whatever system is provided; it is there for your protection. If you live on the ground floor or face a fire escape and are worried about your windows, talk to the superintendent about window locks or security screens. Don't open a door unless you know who is there. Don't admit a salesperson, repairman, or delivery person unless you know or are expecting the person. Many service people carry an identification card issued to them by their companies. Ask to see it.

None of this is meant to frighten you, but it is common sense. If you use the various safeguards that exist, then you can feel secure, relaxed, and protected. If you do not, you are taking a chance almost anywhere nowadays.

If you lock yourself out of your apartment by mistake, the superintendent can let you in again with a master key kept for such emergencies. Some people also leave a spare key with a trusted neighbor for just such moments of need. In most large cities there are locksmiths available on 24-hour duty. Look under "Locksmiths" in the Yellow Pages. They can be lifesavers if, for example, you break off the key in your car lock by mistake.

Fire and Other Emergencies

There are some simple precautions that will help prevent fires. Do not burn trash on your own. Most populated areas of the country have laws that forbid trash burning by individuals. Trash is placed in cans or strong plastic bags for pickup by the garbage collectors. In apartment houses, follow the trash instructions for the building.

Most house fires are caused by burning fat, by defective electrical wiring, or by cigarettes. Never leave your home — even for a minute — while anything is cooking. All homes should have a small foam fire extinguisher near the stove; these are good for either fat or electrical fires. You can buy small portable ones at most hardware stores. Be sure to check the date before you buy — they deteriorate with age. Also, keep a box or two of baking soda handy. It quickly smothers grease or oil flames. Smoke alarms are required by law in most places. They are inexpensive, are easily installed, and are good warnings, especially at night. They are also available in most hardware stores.

As mentioned earlier, in most communities in the United States, the telephone number to call in case of an emergency is 9-1-1. This was mandated by federal law to be completed by late 2003, but in a few communities regular telephone numbers (for fire, police, and ambulance services) are still used and will be listed in a prominent place in the local phone directory (such as the inside front cover). If this is the case, be sure to write the number down and post it on or near the phone. You should use the emergency number for fire, the police, and medical emergencies. You can also dial "0" to get an operator who will connect you to the emergency number. Keep in mind, however, that if you dial an operator (or if you call 9-1-1 on a cell phone), you will not immediately alert officials to your location. The most important thing is to remain calm enough to relay the essential information quickly. Sadly, the nation's 9-1-1 system is not fully funded, resulting in long waits in large urban areas. Furthering the problem is the widespread inappropriate use of the number, tying up the lines with complaints of noisy neighbors and requests for directions. Remember that 9-1-1 is for emergencies, not for general help.

Liability and Homeowners' or Renters' Insurance

You might think this subject need not concern you. Unfortunately, there is a growing need for everyone to carry liability insurance as well as health insurance, because an increasing number of people are claiming high damages after even the simplest and most ordinary of accidents. If someone trips on your front step, or your dog knocks over a child, or your cleaning woman gets burned on your stove, he or she could — and a growing number do — enter a lawsuit against you and claim damages out of all proportion to the accident. Courts assume that everyone is covered by insurance, so they often award far more in damages than would seem reasonable to most of us. If you do *not* carry insurance for such a situation, you could be in serious financial trouble.

The term to use when inquiring is *comprehensive liability*, which is included in a homeowner's policy. An insurance agent will advise you about the proper level of coverage for your income, the size of your family, and so on. Be sure to consult a responsible agent who will not sell you more insurance than you need. Find an agent through your firm, someone you know in a bank, a friend, or a lawyer. When you get the agent's advice, it is a good idea to discuss what has been recommended with a colleague or friend before actually signing any contract. The more the agent tries to rush you, the more cautious you should be.

You should also seek advice on other kinds of insurance according to the value of your possessions and property. If you did not bring any jewelry, fine paintings, or furniture, you may not need to carry such property insurance as fire or theft, but you should discuss this carefully with a knowledgeable person. Generally speaking, you need cover only a few selected, expensive, and irreplaceable possessions (such as jewels, furs, or cameras, for example) for theft. If you are renting an apartment, you can buy an inexpensive renters' insurance policy. If you buy a home, a homeowner's policy is mandatory, and it is probably worth an upgrade of both the liability and the personal property portions. You will need adequate health and accident insurance because medical costs are so high here, and you need auto insurance if you plan to drive.

13
Food and Food Customs

Along with finding a place to stay, finding something to eat is likely to be foremost on your mind when you arrive. Food is very closely linked to culture, and while most Americans might deny it, there is a dominant style of food that is common here. This chapter explores types of restaurants, styles of food, our food habits, and food customs.

Most cities feature inexpensive paperback books, usually available in bookstores, covering their eating places, or you can check local magazines and newspapers for advertisements. Your colleagues at school or work, or hotel personnel, will be glad to offer suggestions, too.

Hotels

Most people start their visit to the United States by staying in a hotel. You will find that hotel restaurants, grills, and lounges are nearly always more expensive than neighborhood restaurants. It is worth wandering up and down the nearby streets to see if you can find something less expensive and more enjoyable. The hotel employees might also suggest nearby restaurants. Coffee shops in a hotel are sometimes less expensive than restaurants.

Restaurants

Because the United States is home to so many different nationalities, you will be able to find almost any kind of restaurant in the large cities. Listings in the Yellow Pages may be by national cuisine or by area of the city or both. Restaurants range widely in price. Many post their menus in the window so you can get an idea of prices before you enter. If not, you may want to ask to see a menu before you are seated, or else just ask about the price range. Appearances from the outside can be deceptive — what looks small and inconspicuous may turn out to be very expensive, or a nicely decorated place may be quite moderate. It works both ways. You can get a good meal for about five to eight dollars in cafeterias or fast-food chains, but in a medium-priced city restaurant you should expect to pay fifteen dollars and up per person — with wine or drinks extra. Prices in big cities go up fast! Beware of state no-smoking laws in all establishments serving food. In most states patrons in restaurants are no longer permitted to smoke — and you will be unpleasantly surprised if you light up (see "Smoking" below).

If you are going to a middle- or upper-level restaurant to dine, telephone ahead for a reservation — the earlier the better. Keep to the time of your reservation or else phone to say you will be late. Good restaurants will not hold reservations for more than a short time. If you are turned away or asked to wait because you have not reserved ahead, don't take it personally. The management has no choice. Fire laws are extremely strict about the number of occupants, and unannounced fire inspections are frequent. No restaurant owner dares overcrowd his or her establishment.

Many mid-level restaurants will not accept reservations and operate on a first-come, first-served basis. The only way to find out if a restaurant takes reservations is to call.

Quick and Cheap

Fast-food chains, coffee shops, delicatessens (delis), lunch counters, and diners offer quick and inexpensive meals. The food and handling are inspected regularly by government officials, so you can usually feel safe about the food, although you are advised to choose a clean-looking place nonetheless. These places are crowded with people at normal mealtimes, particularly over the lunch hour, but if you eat a little early or a little late, you can usually get a seat without waiting too long. They can be found everywhere, are open long hours, and are useful in keeping your food budget down.

Diners are often found on the outskirts of towns. They vary from clean and shiny to rather old and run down. Truck drivers often stop at them because they are likely to have good parking facilities and serve large portions of good food at low prices. Furthermore, there is often an interesting cross section of people in them, especially in the early morning hours when long-distance truck drivers are eating breakfast. Some diners, built from the earliest prefabricated buildings, are remnants of another era. These have fan clubs with elaborate photographic books devoted to them. You do not generally tip at delis, where you serve yourself, or at fast-food restaurants, but you do leave a minimum tip at lunch counters and diners, say 10 to 15 percent.

Fast-food places (where a limited menu is precooked and ready for rapid dispensing and quick consumption) have become very widespread and popular in the United States. Such chains as McDonald's, Kentucky Fried Chicken (KFC), Burger King, Subway, Jack-in-the-Box, Carl's Jr., Taco Bell, and Wendy's cater to millions of people who want quick service and fairly good food in clean, simple surroundings. There is no tipping, though in many cases you are expected to clear your own table and discard your trash in the containers provided. Fast-food shops are especially appealing to children and young people. By and large, these are not places to take a date!

Although not technically fast food, some restaurants provide full service quickly. Chains include Friendly's, Cracker Barrel, International House of Pancakes (called "I-HOP"), Shoney's, Perkins, Bob Evans, and many others. These emphasize breakfast foods, but offer other items as well.

Bars and Pubs

Some American bars are loud, smoky (in some cities, smoking is now prohibited in bars as well as restaurants — see below), and crowded; others are rather dark and meant for quiet conversation. Some bars are now a common meeting place for singles and can be quite lively, with a dance floor and loud music. Some bars cater particularly to gays and lesbians.

Unless you name the brand of alcohol you want, you are likely to get a less expensive "house" brand, which for most people is perfectly acceptable. We don't usually order beer by the pint or half pint, as you would in some countries. Ask for a glass of draft (usually ten to twelve fluid ounces, or one-third of a liter) or a bottle. There are many varieties of American beer, and it is served very cold. Imported beers, ales, and dark beer, are gaining popularity. Japanese, Chinese, and Mexican beer is often available in good restaurants and bars as well.

U.S. whiskey tends to be sweeter, more full-bodied, and cheaper than the whiskeys of Scotland or Ireland. Canadian whiskey is light. The main U.S. whiskeys are bourbon (made from corn) or a blend of several grains, known as "blended whiskey" and often incorrectly called "rye." If you want real rye whiskey, be sure the bartender understands. He or she will generally serve the blended type unless you make your desire clear.

If you like your drink at room temperature, be sure to say "No ice, please." Americans like most of their drinks ice cold.

An increasingly popular type of pub is a "brew house" or microbrewery. These feature a variety of beer and ale styles, some usually made on the premises. There are usually very good restaurants on site as well.

Hours of Meals

It is possible to be served a meal at any hour — including all night — in most large cities and many small ones, though you may have to look around a bit.

Some places offer Sunday "brunch" (or you might be invited to a brunch at someone's home). This is a combination of breakfast and lunch, served about 11:30 or noon for late Sunday sleepers. If you are outside a major city, it may be difficult to find a place that is open after 8:30 or 9:00 P.M., though lunch counters, diners, and fast-food shops usually stay open late.

In people's homes there is considerable variety as to eating times. The main meal is usually served in the evening, except perhaps on Sundays or holidays, when it may be eaten in the afternoon. In cities people often eat dinner about 7:00 or 7:30 P.M. Outside the cities most people dine earlier, at 6:00 or 6:30 P.M., or sometimes even earlier. The hour for cocktail parties is usually 5:00 or 5:30 P.M.

American Food Habits

Generally speaking, American food is considered rather bland by those accustomed to hot or spicy cuisines. Salads are very popular and are served all year round. Many people in this country have become weight and calorie conscious and are trying to keep down their weight. This is evident in menus offering low calorie (or in many cases, low carbohydrate) or "weight watchers" meals. Grocery stores now offer a huge array of low-fat, "light," no-fat, or "low-carb" foods, from ice cream to soup to snack foods. "Diet" drinks (meaning without sugar but full of artificial sweeteners) such as ginger ale or cola are also popular. If you do not want low-calorie items, read the labels carefully to avoid disappointing choices.

Waiters in restaurants tend to assume that everyone drinks coffee, especially at breakfast and after dinner, but you do not have to do so! Some people drink coffee (regular or decaffeinated) or tea with their meal; others drink wine or just water. When dining out, you can ask for tea, milk, soda, beer, wine, or water if you prefer these to coffee. Restaurants cannot serve beer, wine, or liquor unless they are licensed to do so. Normally, when eating in a home, it is considered polite to drink whatever is being served and not to ask for something different — unless the host gives you a choice or unless you prefer water.

The main course in American meals is usually meat, fowl, or fish, but rarely is more than one of these served at the same meal (except that seafood can be used as an appetizer — shrimp cocktail, steamed clams, pickled herring, or smoked oysters, for example).

Most Americans eat quickly during the day — that is, breakfast and lunch — unless it is a social, business, or family occasion. Racing through daytime meals is part of the fast pace described earlier. Lunch breaks at work are limited to a half hour or an hour. There is also another reason for eating fast — others in public eating places are waiting for you to finish so they too can be served and get back to work on time. Each one hurries to make room for the next person. The evening meal, however, is usually leisurely and a family time — unless, of course, there are children (especially teenagers) involved in sports or other late-afternoon activities.

There is a real difference in leisure and timing here between a meal that is "social," meaning shared and enjoyed, and one that is "just a meal."

The Language of Food

The terms used in ordering or buying food can lead to fulfilled expectations or surprises. Use the wrong words and your coffee may turn into liquid candy or your entrée burned beyond recognition.

Meat

If you order steaks, roast beef, hamburgers, prime rib, and so on, the waiter may say, "How would you like it?" meaning whether you want your meat rare, medium, or well done. If you order it rare, the meat will be red inside; if medium, it will be pink; if well done, it will be completely cooked (and sometimes dry).

"Rare" is likely to be cooked just a little; "well done" to be very well cooked. If you prefer, you can indicate something in the middle by saying "medium rare" or "medium well."

Coffee

If you order coffee or tea, the waiter will sometimes ask, "Would you like cream?" If you would not, answer "Just black, please," meaning no cream or sugar. Sugar is generally already on the table, and often milk or cream is also, and the waiter brings the coffee black. Many people now ask for "decaf," meaning decaffeinated coffee. In New York City, "regular" coffee means liberal amounts of both cream and sugar. Elsewhere, it merely refers to coffee that hasn't been decaffeinated.

Coffee is a popular American drink at all hours of the day. It varies enormously in quality; you will just have to experiment to find places that make it the way you like it. Espresso and other specialties are often available, but you have to ask for them. Coffee-house chain stores, such as Starbuck's, Peet's, and Seattle Coffee Roasters, have sprung up in nearly every American city. These offer heartier, darker coffee than traditional American coffee, and a dizzying array of "specialty" coffee drinks as well as pastries and other food. A variety of kinds of tea is also available in these shops.

Tea

Tea is much less popular than coffee in the United States. It is often quite tasteless; perhaps we make it poorly because we don't drink it as much as other nationalities do. In public places tea is usually a shock to the newcomer. A cup of hot water (no longer boiling if it ever was) is brought in with a tea bag in the saucer. You are supposed to put the bag into the water and leave it there until the tea is as strong as you like it. In private homes you will sometimes find it brewed. Herb teas have also become popular in the United States.

Other Drinks

Next after coffee, Americans are likely to drink Coke or other soft drinks, milk, or fruit juices. Iced tea is usually good and is very popular in summer, as is iced coffee. Both can be served either sweetened or unsweetened, although unfortunately not often at the same place. If you want to drink water, you may have to ask for it, except in the more expensive restaurants. Tap water is safe anywhere, but you can request bottled water if you prefer the taste.

Eggs

The waiter at a restaurant will ask you, "How do you want your eggs?" Your answer can include any one of a wide range of possibilities: boiled, fried, scrambled, or poached; with or without ham or bacon or sausage. You also indicate the number of eggs you want. Most Americans consider one or two eggs normal. Boiled eggs are emptied into a cup — rarely, if ever, eaten out of the shell. Fried eggs may be "sunny-side up," meaning fried on one side only (with the yellow face showing); "over," meaning well fried on both sides; or "over easy," meaning fried lightly on both sides.

The addition of one or two slices of bacon, ham, or sausage may be quite expensive. Take a look at the price on the menu before ordering. Usually a listed breakfast is less expensive than ordering side dishes.

French Fries and Coleslaw

French fries are fried potatoes — usually sliced thinly like Belgian fritte, but sometimes they are sliced into wedges more like British "chips." You often get them with a meal whether you order them or not. The same is true of coleslaw — sliced cabbage and mayonnaise. If these are served with the meal, there is no extra charge for them.

Hot Dogs and Hamburgers

Usually hot dogs (frankfurters) are eaten in a long bread roll. The meat can be either beef or pork. You have your choice of adding tomato ketchup (spiced tomato sauce), mustard, pickle, relish, or onion (chopped and raw). Some people put all of these on at once! There is no charge for such condiments.

Hamburgers are one of the few purely American dishes. They are the staple of the fast-food chains (McDonald's, for example) and vary significantly in quality from restaurant to restaurant. They are supposed to be made of pure beef, with varying percentages of fat, though sometimes soybeans are mixed in with the meat. In both restaurants and fast-food places, unless you specify what you *don't* want, your burger usually comes with lettuce, tomato, onion, pickle, and a mayonnaise-type sauce.

Smoking

Smoking is now prohibited in restaurants in much of the country. No doubt the days of a cigarette between courses or at the end of a meal will someday be gone forever, which you may find refreshing or stifling depending on your feelings about smoking. The original rationale for these bans was health concerns about second-hand smoke, which is supported by some research studies but refuted by others. In reality, public support for these restrictions is high because fewer people smoke, and nonsmokers have become accustomed to (some would say self-righteous about) their right to cleaner air.

In the 1970s, restaurants were required to provide nonsmoking sections, which were typically small rooms or even just a few tables. Gradually, the non-smoking areas became larger and the smokers were banished to smaller tables. In many restaurants, even in locales without legal bans, smoking is not permitted at all on the premises.

Obesity

Although not yet technically considered a disease in its own right, obesity is nonetheless an epidemic in the United States. According to the American

Obesity Association, the rate of obesity in the United States roughly doubled between 1970 and 2000, to over a third of all adults. Even more alarming is the rate of childhood obesity, although these increases are partly due to a 1998 change in the way obesity is calculated. According to the U.S. Bureau of the Census, in 2003[1] Americans ate an average of twenty-five pounds of candy each! Our love affair with the automobile, along with road construction that is decidedly bicycle/pedestrian-hostile, has made it difficult (and in some cases impossible) in many areas to walk from one place to another. Combined with the plethora of television programming and the rise of video games, the reality is that we get very little simple exercise. Amazingly, some people will go so far as to drive one or two miles to a gym in order to walk on a treadmill!

In addition, many foods are extraordinarily high in fat content, and our portions are quite large by almost any standard. Although some fast-food places have recently discontinued "super-size" from their menus, the "large" size is quite large enough. The fat content of many menu items is increased without noticeably increasing serving size. It is not just hamburgers, however, that should be viewed with caution. During that same period, one chain's small vanilla shake doubled its fat content. Another fast-food chain increased the saturated fat content of its french fries by 60 percent.

Fast-food giants gear their marketing toward children, hoping to develop loyal customers who will prefer the particular taste of their food items. According to Eric Schlosser in his book *Fast Food Nation*,[3] McDonald's operates more playgrounds than any other private entity and is one of the largest distributors of toys in the United States. It uses a clown (who is depicted in advertisements as a child's one true friend) as its spokesman.

Not all overweight people are obese. In order to be considered obese, a person must exceed a body mass index (BMI) of 30, which is a ratio of body fat to height. This ratio, however, fails to distinguish between fat and muscle, differences in bone density, and other factors when determining whether a person is overwieght. Nonetheless, the social costs of obesity are high — lost productivity, increased healthcare costs, and shorter life spans can all be attributed to obesity. Each year, *Men's Fitness* magazine publishes an index of the fattest cities in the United States. While Detroit came in first in 2004, five of the top eight — Houston, Dallas, San Antonio, Fort Worth, and Arlington — are in Texas.

Health Food

Fortunately, there is a counter-trend to combat obesity. In the past decade, there has been a rise in the availability of healthier food in the form of organic (grown without pesticides or herbicides) produce and whole foods. Every city has at least one healthfood store, and there are even some supermarket chains (e.g., Freshfields, Wild Oats, Bread and Circus) that specialize in healthier, although costlier, food. Organic food is more widely available than ever before, often found at regular supermarkets as well as at specialty stores. There is also a "slow-food" movement to counter the prevalence of fast food. Begun in Italy in 1986, there about 80,000 members of Slow Food International worldwide (about half of them in Italy), a nonprofit organization designed to preserve and support the pleasures of the table. The international movement was founded in Paris in 1989, and Slow Food boasts more than 70 chapters throughout the United States. Consult www.slowfoodusa.org/ for information on a chapter near you.

The same *Men's Fitness* survey mentioned above also names the fittest cities in the U.S.: Honolulu, San Francisco, Virginia Beach, Denver, Colorado Springs, Seattle, Boston, Portland (Oregon), and Tucson topped the 2004 list in this category.

14

Staying in Touch with People

Recent years have seen a communication revolution. New digital technology, including the Internet, satellite communications, and fiber optics make getting your message — around the block or around the world — faster and, in most cases, cheaper. Still the old-fashioned ways are not yet displaced completely, and you will surely want to write a letter sooner or later.

Postal Service

The U.S. Postal Service is sometimes criticized by Americans for losing mail and for being slow, especially in the large cities, where millions of pieces are handled daily. Deliveries are made once a day, but not on Sundays. Despite rising costs, however, the Postal Service remains one of our country's greatest bargains. The same stamp that carries your letter across town will just as inexpensively carry it across the country. There are still places in the U.S. where mail is delivered by airplane, and at least one village in the Grand Canyon receives its mail by pack mule! One quirk of the English language to keep in mind is that in the U.S., the *Postal* Service brings the *mail* (unlike in England, where the Royal *Mail* brings the *post!*).

There are often long lines at post offices, so it is a good idea to buy books of stamps or rolls of stamps to avoid frequent trips to the post office. For ordinary mail within the United States, buy a supply of first-class stamps; for overseas, buy a supply of air-letter forms or lightweight stationery and appropriate stamps. The cost for overseas postage varies from country to country, so you will have to ask. If you have these supplies for your normal daily needs, you can then drop your letters into the nearest mailbox and avoid standing in long lines at the post office. Remember, though, to have your letter weighed if you suspect it is over the allotted weight. If you must go to the post office, try to avoid the lunch hour and the four to five o'clock rush when every mailing clerk in the city is bringing in the day's office mail.

In the United States, zip codes follow the name of the city and state; they do not precede the city as in Europe, South America, and other places. The proper format within the U.S. is as follows:

Your Name
Street Address
City, State, Zip Code

> Recipient's Name
> Street Address
> City, State, Zip Code

Most post offices offer post office boxes, which can be rented for a period of months. You will be given a key or combination to pick up your mail. This can be very convenient if your stay will be short or if you move several times during your stay.

Remember to put your mail on "hold" while you are away for vacation or business, and to forward it when you move. This will prevent someone from intercepting your mail (and gaining access to your credit card and bank account numbers). Ask for instructions on how to do so at any post office.

Sending Money by Mail

If you want to send money abroad by mail, be sure to ask for an international postal money order. You must clearly specify that you want an *international* form.

Types of Mail Service

Inside the United States, all first-class mail is shipped by air without extra cost. An airmail indication is not needed on the envelope. If you want to be sure an important letter has been received, send it certified or ask for delivery confirmation. Be aware that certified mail travels more slowly, as it must be logged at each station along the way. For extra cost, it is possible to use express mail for overnight delivery.

The post office is only one of a growing number of express delivery companies, and prices for an overnight letter vary.

Packages

There are many rules and regulations governing the mailing of packages. Permissible sizes and weights vary. Double-check before mailing anything that is potentially explosive or flammable; it may be permitted but will likely require special labeling and handling (for example, sent overland rather than by air). Tape is now used to secure parcels instead of string, which used to catch in the postal machines. You can buy strong packing tape in stationery stores, most supermarkets, pharmacies, and at the post office. Note that if you send something priority or express mail, the post office provides a variety of boxes for free.

There are special rates (called media mail) for books and printed matter. Ask the postal clerk about them. If you are sending books overseas, ask about surface and air postage rates.

United Parcel Service (UPS), Federal Express, and other commercial services are taking over much of the package delivery service within the United States and overseas, being both cheaper and quicker than the postal service in many cases. It is worth calling them for any large packages (check the phone book). You can drop your package off in designated locations or have the company pick it up from your house or office; they charge for doing so.

Telephones

Almost everyone in the United States uses the telephone to conduct business, to chat with friends, to make or break social engagements, to shop (catalogue companies are flooding the mail delivery system, encouraging the customer to phone in purchases by credit card), and to obtain all kinds of information. Telephones save your feet and endless amounts of time — not to mention multiple bus or subway fares. It is the chief means of communication in the United States. People are also increasingly relying on fax machines and e-mail (see "E-mail and Internet Access" later in this chapter) to send information to another person or to a business.

Some visitors from other countries hesitate to telephone at first because they are afraid that they will be bothering the other person. Within normal hours — after 8:30 in the morning and before 9:00 at night — people are used to the telephone ringing and will not mind at all. Most offices have an employee whose job it is to answer the phone from 9 A.M. to 5 P.M. You need never worry about calling a business concern for information, nor will you find them closed at lunchtime, though of course a particular individual may be out. It can be confusing at first to place a call. Our telephone numbers consist of ten digits (for example, (555) 555-5555). The first three digits, usually in parentheses, comprise the area code. Within the same area code, the local seven-digit number is usually sufficient; however, many large cities have several area codes, so you must dial all ten digits. When calling long distance, you will need to precede the call with a "1" and include the area code. To make it more confusing, in some low-density places, a single area code will encompass many small cities (or even an entire state), some of which are a long-distance call from one another!

If you do not wish to receive sales calls, you can request that your telephone number be placed on the national "Do-Not-Call" list through the Internet at www.donotcall.gov/. This list subjects telemarketers to a $500 penalty, payable to you, if they disregard your wishes on this matter.

It is simple and quick to have a phone installed. Just call the business office of the local telephone company (see the front of the local telephone directory). They will install it on a specific day by appointment, when it is convenient for you. You must be at home to tell them where you want the phone to be placed. Unfortunately, sometimes the process is much more expensive for students, who may have to make a large deposit to initiate service.

There are a number of companies that offer long-distance services. AT&T, MCI, and Sprint are among the largest. There are also a great many stores that offer a vast array of phones to buy. Don't overlook discount stores if your needs are not extravagant.

You will be charged a basic monthly rate by your local telephone company. It can be quite confusing to select your carriers. Usually, there is a monopoly that handles your local calls. If you do not anticipate making many calls in your immediate area, you may opt for a lower monthly fee but a per-charge call (even for calling next door!) or you can choose a higher monthly fee that includes unlimited local calling. Next you can choose a company to provide your regional long-distance calls — these are outside your city but include cities near you. Finally, you need a long-distance carrier for calling across the country. You may choose your local telephone company for all of these services, but you may not receive the lowest rates in doing so. There is fierce competition among long-distance companies, and they offer a wide variety of plans including reduced international charges and free calls to specific numbers. Some of these special "calling plans" have a per-month fee attached to them.

Independent of these choices are the many "per-call" long-distance companies, through which you place calls by dialing a separate code preceding your call (for example, 10-10-220). When you do so, that company, and not your regular carrier, will bill your call. You may want to ask some American colleagues for advice — even *we* get confused about all the choices. Beware of sales calls from many of the telephone companies. They may offer "bargains" that actually cost you more money!

Telephone Directories

When your telephone is installed, you will be given two directories — the regular directory, in which names of people with phones are listed alphabetically, and the Yellow Pages. In smaller cities, these are often in one book. It is worthwhile to sit down and really study these books when you first get them. They contain a great deal of information about using the telephone, special services that are available (including time, weather, or traffic information), rates, times of the week when you can phone most cheaply, area codes, state zip codes, and so on. The Yellow Pages lists all businesses, organizations, restaurants, stores, and services in your area in such a way that you can quickly find whatever you need. If you study that directory, you will learn much about your city and the range of what is available: schools, clubs, organizations, public swimming pools, all kinds of instruction and classes, information about where to buy special foods or spices; shops for all sorts of goods; restaurants by nationality; and places where you can rent furniture, television sets, stereos, children's cribs, crutches, or a wide range of articles (look under "Rental Service").

The Yellow Pages, which is updated every year, can become one of your best friends if you take the trouble to get to know it well.

Telephone Credit Cards

As soon as you select your telephone company and have your own number, you can call the business office and ask for a credit card. This is free and is a great convenience, enabling you to make calls from any telephone, public or private, and have the call charged to your home account. This often saves you from having to struggle with exact change in a telephone booth, particularly for a long-distance call, and makes it possible to call from a friend's home or office without imposing on his or her generosity. Be careful about using your card very often; the charge for doing so can be shockingly high.

Public Telephones

Public telephones here are still widespread, but they are not as easy to find as they once were due to the popularity of cell phones. You will find public phones in bus and air terminals, railroad stations, stores, hotels, the lobbies of many office buildings, restaurants, gasoline stations, and in small booths along streets and highways. Instructions for use are found on each phone. Long-distance and overseas calls can also be made from public telephones, but you must have either a telephone credit card or a handful of change in nickels, dimes, and quarters; sometimes you can bill calls to a regular credit card. If you would like the recipient to pay the charges, ask the operator to make it a "collect" call or say you wish to reverse the charges. All operator services cost extra.

Answering Machines and Voice Mail

Answering machines are now so popular that you will find your colleagues and friends upset if you don't have one on your private phone as well as on your business phone. You will hear a message indicating that the person you called is not available and inviting you to leave a message at the "sound of the tone." This may seem to be a very impersonal practice, but it allows busy people to receive or deliver messages and return calls. Answering machines can be purchased from any store selling phones. Remember, though, that with both message machines and phones, you generally get what you pay for, so avoid the least expensive sets. Voice mail is a service that provides you with a personal mailbox for your telephone messages. Rather than a machine in your home, your messages are recorded by your telephone company and can be retrieved from home or from another phone by using a pass-code.

Cellular (Mobile) Phones

As in many countries, cell phones proliferate here. There are a myriad of options available to you, including "pay-as-you-go" plans and flat rates for unlimited calls at specific times or to specific numbers. The same companies that offer residential telephone service offer cellular service, along with Cingular, Cellular 1, and T-Mobile, among others. While you will undoubtedly see people doing it, it is considered rude to chat on the telephone in restaurants and other public places. Some busy commuter trains now offer "phone-free" sections.

Telegrams and Cables

Within the United States you may send a telegram or a mailgram, although both have been virtually eliminated by e-mail and cell phones. You send cables and telegrams by telephoning The Western Union Company or visiting a Western Union office. You can also send and receive money by cable.

E-Mail and Internet Access

Electronic mail (e-mail) and, increasingly, instant messaging (IM) are fast becoming the communication method of choice, especially among young people. In order to connect your home computer to the World Wide Web, you need to first select an Internet Service Provider (ISP). Popular choices include Earthlink, American Online (AOL), and Microsoft Network (MSN), along with a myriad of others, including cable television and telephone companies. You have four possible choices, although all of them are not available in all areas.

Dial-Up

The least expensive is to use your regular phone line to dial an ISP using your computer's built-in modem. For somewhere less than half to a third of the monthly charge of the other options, dial-up is limited in speed to 56 kilobits per second and can be excruciatingly slow for heavy users, especially if you want to view lots of images on the Web. It is also inconvenient in that you cannot place or receive telephone calls while your computer is connected.

DSL

This uses your regular phone line but does not prevent you from placing or receiving voice calls at the same time. It operates far faster than dial-up, but it is more costly and requires special equipment to connect your computer's network port to the phone line, although many companies waive the equipment charge when you sign a one-year contract.

Cable

This is very similar in speed and price to DSL but is carried through the television cable rather than the telephone line. There is also special equipment involved, but again it is sometimes free with an annual contract agreement.

Satellite

If you have satellite television, you can access the Internet that way instead of using wires. This is more expensive than cable or DSL, has more equipment charges, and is generally slower.

Once you have decided on an ISP, you can use the company's services to provide you with an e-mail account. Most ISPs also include some storage space for a personal Web server or file transfer protocol (ftp) server, which can be handy for storing files you wish to access from another computer. If you don't have a computer, you can buy an inexpensive (Under $100) e-mail machine and pay a lesser monthly amount for e-mail-only access (these machines are sometimes discounted or even free when you sign a one-year contract). Or you can use public-access computers in many libraries for free. You can get a free e-mail account through many web portals such as Yahoo! (www.yahoo.com) or Hotmail (www.hotmail.com).

Wireless Access Points (WAPs)

Airport lounges, coffee shops, and other public locations are increasingly offering access to wireless networks, which usually use the 802.11(b) standard, although the faster (and mutually compatible) 802.11(g) is increasingly available. The charge for this access is usually by the hour.

15
Transportation

Americans move around a city on foot or by bus, taxi, car, or (in some cities) subway (sometimes called the metro) — just as is done in cities the world over. The rules for doing so, however, are different in every country.

On Foot

If distances are short, the quickest way to get from one place to another may be on foot. Traffic in our cities and towns is often very heavy, particularly during morning and evening rush hours at the beginning and ending of the workday. So city people often get to their destination most quickly on foot if distances permit. Many people also walk as a form of exercise.

Jaywalking, which means either crossing in the middle of a block or crossing against the traffic light, is illegal in most communities, and you could be fined if caught. You will see many people taking chances, but do not follow their example. It is not worth it. Most pedestrian injuries are the result of jaywalking.

If you come from a country where driving is on the left, be especially careful to look *both* ways for oncoming cars and have your children practice doing the same. Many people are hurt by failing to do this before stepping off the curb. Unlike in London, our cities do not have helpful signs reminding people that the traffic may be coming from the opposite direction from what they are accustomed to or expecting. The widespread use of one-way streets makes it advisable for everyone to be extra cautious about crossing our city streets.

By Bus

Trams or trolley cars are now rarely found in U.S. cities; generally the public travels by bus or subway. More and more cities are requiring passengers to have the exact change in hand as they board the bus — or else "tokens" (small coin-like pieces similar to the French *jeton*) that can be bought in advance. Drivers used to have the double job of making change at the same time that they were driving their huge buses through traffic. The exact-change rule eases the driver's work and speeds service for everyone. It also reduces the number of robberies that were taking place when drivers had a great deal of extra money for making change.

In many cities bus and subway tokens can be used interchangeably and are bought at subway booths. It is a great time saver to buy tokens in considerable quantity and keep them in a special purse or envelope so that you can get at them easily. Otherwise, you may have to wait in long lines during rush hour or get caught without change just when you need to catch a bus. If you are using two buses (or a subway and a bus) to reach your destination, you can request a "transfer," a small slip of paper that allows you to pay one fare for the entire trip but use two (or sometimes more) vehicles to complete your trip.

Bus stops are usually located at busy corners and are clearly marked. Normally, the bus schedule is displayed at the stop, and in most cities you can request printed bus schedules from the bus driver or company. In some cities you can telephone to ask for the best route to go from one point to another, and most have Websites with printable maps and schedules. If time allows, the bus driver will often give quick directions or at least tell you when to get off the bus.

Schoolchildren and people over sixty-five years of age can get special passes in most cities so that they can ride at reduced rates during certain hours of the day.

By Subway (or Metro)

Subways, or metros, in some cities are by far the quickest way to move about. Networks of them lie under a number of our cities, and they operate day and night. Most of the time they are filled with people and can be used safely. There are a few warnings, however, that should be observed.

1. Naturally, avoid rush hours if you can. Subways are full from about 7:30 to 9:30 A.M. and again from about 4:30 to 6:00 or 6:30 P.M. (These are the hours when pickpockets do their best work, too.)

2. Choose to sit in cars where there are other people, rather than empty ones.

3. For safety while waiting for a train, stand near the token booth if possible.

4. Hold your purse firmly and consciously — don't let it dangle. Men should carry wallets in inside jacket pockets.

5. Before riding the subway at night, ask a friend or colleague whether it is safe and whether there are areas of the city that should be avoided at night.

Subway or metro stops are clearly marked, and maps of the system are available at most stations. In some cities, the fare varies with the length of your trip and in others a flat fee takes you anywhere in the system. Increasingly city transit systems are doing away with tokens (special coins) and using fare cards instead. With fare cards, passengers usually pay by the distance traveled. You buy a card in a machine at a subway or metro station, and slide it into a turnstile or gate machine at the entrance. Your card is read, and you slide it once more when you exit the station at your destination. The fare is then deducted from the remaining value of the card. Save yourself trouble by buying tokens (or fare cards) in quantity if you plan to use subways regularly. Many cities also offer discounted daily, weekly, or monthly passes.

It is helpful to have a basic understanding of the system's navigation cues before you start. In Manhattan, for example, trains run generally either "uptown" (north) or "downtown" (south) before continuing on to other boroughs such as Queens or Brooklyn. In contrast, Boston's metro system (called the "T") labels trains either "inbound" (toward Government Center and Park Street stations) or "outbound," meaning away from them in either direction. Thus it is important to know if your destination lies between these points or away from them.

By Taxi

Because at first they feel uncertain, most people are likely to travel by taxi (also called cabs) when they arrive in any new place. Here, taxis definitely come under the heading of luxury travel. Furthermore, taxis have an aggravating way of being hard to find, not only at the busy hours of a day but also if the weather turns bad. In most cities you can telephone to get one (see the local phone book for numbers); but in others, including New York, you usually hail them on the street or find them at a "hack stand" (special parking areas reserved for taxis).

Generally speaking, taxis are metered throughout the country, but there are some cities (e.g., Washington, D.C.) where they operate on a distance zone system. Nothing is uniform in the United States. You will need to ask a friend, a colleague, or hotel personnel about the rules; they vary from city to city. Also be sure to use a well-known taxi company to avoid being overcharged.

Although drivers do not always comply, the regulations are as follows: they must stop if the taxi is empty and not showing an off-duty sign; they must drive anywhere within the city limits; they may not ask your destination before you get in and then refuse to take you; and they may not charge more than is registered on the meter except for trunks, for bridge, tunnel, or ferry tolls, or for late-night special fees. Off-duty signs are often indicated by lights on the taxi roof, but it is wise to ask someone how to tell when a taxi is off duty and can therefore be expected to pass you by. It varies from city to city.

There are various sizes of cabs. Often they are not permitted to carry more than four people — sometimes as few as three — but some can carry five or six passengers. If you find yourself sharing a cab with several strangers (legal in some cities but not in others), you will often be expected to pay full price, unfair though that may seem.

In heavily congested areas the driver may not be allowed by law to get out of the cab to open doors or help with luggage. Do not assume the driver is being discourteous — it may be a safety measure.

If you want to make a complaint about taxi service, note the driver's number and name (posted somewhere inside the cab). Be sure to get the name of the taxi company also — there are many companies in all cities. When you write to the company, be sure to keep a copy of your letter.

By Car

Americans' love affair with the automobile is legendary, even notorious. If you live in a large city, you may very well be able to avoid the hassle and expense of owning a car. Also, many college towns and enlightened small cities (such as Portland, Oregon) are still accessible by foot or public transportation. But poor regional planning has made it difficult, or even impossible, for anyone living in most of the country to get around comfortably without a motorized vehicle.

Costs

Owning a car in any U.S. city is expensive. In addition to the original cost of the car, one has to pay heavy insurance premiums. Rates vary by city and by coverage, but one can pay substantial amounts in insurance alone in congested cities. In addition, the car must be registered and licensed (fee depends on the weight or type of car). The cost of a driver's license must be added to that. The price of gasoline, although low by world standards, is still substantial, and parking costs are often *very* high, particularly in large cities.

There are no customs or other duty charges on a private imported car if it is shipped home again within one year; however, if you sell it in the United States within a year, you will have to pay duty — based on the appraised value of the car at the time of import. *Be sure* to bring your registration papers or proof of ownership. This is very important. Check with your nearest U.S. consulate or with your local automobile club on the latest rulings and charges before you come. There are also strict regulations regarding the pollution emissions of cars. Your car will have to be adapted to conform to these rules. This can be prohibitively expensive for foreign cars.

In many states, a car tax is added to the registration fee (done once a year), the amount dependent on the age and make of the car. Also, most states require an inspection once a year or every six months to determine that the car is safe to drive.

Licensing

If you bring your car to the U.S., you get an international registration marker for it before leaving home. You will be allowed to drive to your destination with your national license plates or tags, but immediately on arrival you must obtain American license plates from the state in which you will be living. Each state has its own Department (or Registry) of Motor Vehicles (see your local telephone directory for the address), which issues both license and registration. Motorists may have to take a test and secure a U.S. driver's license unless they come from a country that is party to the International Convention on Road Traffic (1949) or the Inter-American Convention (1943), in which case they must carry an international driving permit. In many states, you are required to obtain a local driver's license immediately (or within 30 or 90 days) of taking up residence. If you buy a car in the United States, you must obtain a driver's license for the state where you live within a set time. And if you move to another state, you must do the same. Since regulations are complicated and vary somewhat from state to state, play it safe and call the Department of Motor Vehicles in your town or city to inquire about licensing and license plates.

Bring lots of documentation; requirements for issuing driver's licenses have become more onerous since September 11, 2001. Department of Motor Vehicle personnel commonly insist on seeing passports, notices from the Bureau of Citizenship and Immigration Services, Social Security cards, and proof of local addresses.

It is also wise to have at least a few hours of professional instruction *no matter how well you drive,* to learn rules of the road, local requirements, and, especially, American "driving psychology." Brazilian, Greek, Japanese, and French drivers all behave differently behind a wheel; so do Americans. Just as important are the informal road rules that vary from city to city. Etiquette for passing and merging is different in Boston and New York; both are very different from that in Portland, Oregon, or Portland, Maine.

Each state's Department of Motor Vehicles will give you a free booklet, upon request, covering state rules. It is important to remember: *ignorance of the law is never considered an excuse* if you run into trouble. You are expected to learn the law and abide by it when you drive.

Automobile Insurance

It is imperative that you protect yourself with liability insurance (covering damage to the other person), and you should insure yourself at a substantial level, not the minimum. If you should hit someone, damages charged here can be astronomically high. Lawyers assume that insurance companies (not the individual) will pay, so they ask damage fees accordingly. If you are *not* covered, you can be financially ruined by gigantic fees charged for injury, fright, shock, or other complaints — even if the accident appeared to you to be slight. Not everyone presses such suits, but enough people do so that you need to be well protected. Although insurance is costly, it is absolutely necessary and is legally required in most of the country. Insurance premiums vary, depending on the age and sex of the driver, the type of car, and the geographic area; premiums for young, single men who own sports cars are extremely high.

Buying a Car

Barring any strikes or emergency delays, you receive delivery on a new car quite quickly in this country. American manufacturers are still building cars with high horsepower and low mileage per gallon of gas. Sport utility vehicles (SUVs) as well as small cars, both American- and foreign-made (or a combination thereof) are also very popular. In general, foreign cars are easy to obtain and to keep repaired, although repair and parts may be more expensive. Hybrid vehicles — ones that run on a combination of electricity and traditional gasoline — are gaining popularity. Very few cars in the U.S. use diesel fuel, but if you do get one, be extremely careful to use the correct fuel when refilling (see "Service Stations" later in this section for more details).

Don't buy a car at what is called "list price" until you have talked to a number of people about it. Automobiles are perhaps the one commodity in the United States where haggling is still expected. Prices can usually be "bargained down" and can vary considerably among dealerships. Prices also fluctuate markedly from one month to another, depending on how close it is to the appearance of new models. If you buy in the fall, just before the new models become available, dealers are trying to get rid of last year's models, and you can get a good bargain as a result. Ask and explore; don't buy too fast. There are very good Websites (www.cars.com/ and www.edmunds.com/ are two of them) that can be extremely informative about how much you should expect to pay for a particular vehicle.

Car dealers make their greatest profit in two ways: (1) on extras and (2) on arranging the financing and insurance.

Extras. Extras are the multitude of optional features, which all dealers try hard to sell: radios, cassette players, special paint color, air conditioning, fancy seat covers, extended warranties, sunroofs, and other items that are not standard. Dealers are skilled at selling these items, but *you do not need to buy them.* If you are persuaded by a clever salesperson, you may end up paying a considerable amount of money for features that you will not need.

Financing and Insuring. Dealers normally charge higher interest rates than banks when they arrange the terms of financing. Over the months or years of payment, this can be a considerable amount. Look into alternative possibilities *before* you buy. Generally, you will do better to take out your own bank loan rather than work through a car dealer, who, after all, must take his or her share, and then work with a bank anyway. Dealers will do their best to persuade you to finance the car through them, but it is not required. Don't feel obligated.

Secondhand Cars

The drop in value of American cars after a year or two is so great that many people buy used cars rather than new ones. Prices depend on the age of the car, its condition, its size and make, the area of the country where it is bought, and the time of year. Here are two suggestions that will help you:

1. Be especially careful when buying a secondhand car that is older than four years.

2. Never go alone. Take someone with you who not only knows cars well but also knows the ways of American dealers.

Often it is an advantage to go to an area where wealthy people live to find your car. They turn their cars in more often than less affluent people, and the cars are normally in good condition.

Used-car dealers vary widely as to reliability; try to deal with one that has been recommended to you. Generally speaking, your chances will be better with a reputable dealer (one that represents one or more specific brands of new cars) than at a used-car lot, though you will see a lot of these outside most big cities.

Many people do their buying outside city limits for a couple of reasons. The dealer's reputation is at stake in a small town, so he or she tends to be more careful than in the anonymity of a large city. Second, a smaller dealer may be more motivated to sell a car. However, do not think that you can avoid paying sales tax by buying in another location. Sales taxes are usually assessed when you register the car, and it is based on your residence, not the location of the dealer. Many people buy used cars without going through a dealer at all. Classified advertisements in newspapers and on the Internet can help you find a bargain. Be aware, however, that there are fewer buyer protections for a privately arranged sale.

It takes time and trouble to buy a secondhand car. If you do not have a friend or colleague who knows cars well, take a garage mechanic whom you trust with you. It is worth what you have to pay for his or her time. Many mechanics are glad to do such consulting work after hours or on weekends. Determine the price of this service in advance, however.

Be sure you actually *drive* the car before buying. You will be allowed to do so. If you haven't brought a mechanic with you, take the car to a nearby garage and ask the mechanic to test it out and give you an opinion as to its condition. There are certain key points he will look for that will give him a quick idea of the car's general condition. It is worth paying something for a careful examination by a mechanic whom you trust. Do this *before* you sign any papers. Before you buy any car — new or used — talk to people at your office or college or to any friends you have made. There are various tricks of the trade that you should know.

Another way to arrange an inspection of a used car is for you to arrange to pay a mechanic for the car directly; he or she is therefore working for you. The seller then takes the car to the mechanic at a convenient time, avoiding the hassle of your trying to juggle three schedules — yours, the seller's and the mechanic's — to do this yourself.

Leasing a Car

Leasing has become quite popular in the United States. It can be a particularly attractive option if you plan to live in the United States for only a few years and don't want the trouble of having to sell a car before you leave. Typically, leases last for two to three years, during which time you make monthly payments. At the end of the lease, you simply return the car to the original dealer with no remaining obligations. Lease rates tend to be high, though, and most dealers require you to carry extra insurance.

Leasing has two major drawbacks. First, if you decide you don't want to keep the car for the duration of the lease and wish to return it early, you may be obligated to pay the dealer the difference in the value of the car from the date you first leased it to the date you return it. Second, if you exceed the number of miles stated in the original contract, you will be charged a penalty per mile. These can sometimes add up to thousands of dollars. If you're sure you will keep the car for a set period of time and can predict the distance you will travel, however, a lease is an option to consider.

Renting a Car

With street parking so difficult, parking rates so high, and streets so crowded, increasing numbers of city dwellers find owning a car in the city not worth the effort. Instead, they use public transportation within the city and rent a car only when they need one for out-of-town trips or vacations. Most overseas visitors are likely to find this by far the cheapest and easiest method, too. There are many rental companies everywhere. You can rent by the day, week, month, or year.

If you work in the United States, your own firm may have a special discount arrangement with a particular rental agency — companies often do. It is worth asking about this at work. Some agencies have had bad experiences and will not rent to individuals from abroad because of past insurance difficulties or problems with payments. On the other hand, other agencies give additional discounts to visitors from abroad as a special courtesy. You will need to explore a bit and make inquiries.

Costs are usually determined by length of rental time and size of car. Insurance is extra. However, there are other options: some agencies also charge by mileage, others do not; some require that you return the car to its starting point, others will rent cars for one-way travel between cities, although the cost for one-way rentals may be considerably higher.

Driving Under the Influence of Alcohol or Other Drugs

The United States is trying to stop drunken driving — as are many other countries. Still, nearly 20,000 people a year in the U.S. are killed annually in alcohol-related crashes — nearly half of all traffic deaths. State laws vary on this, but police can stop drivers and require them to take breath or blood tests in many states if they suspect the driver of being under the influence of alcohol. Penalties vary from state to state: fines for a first offense, overnight (or longer) imprisonment, suspension of license, and/or, in some areas, required community service (working as assistants in hospitals or nursing homes, for instance), or alcohol counseling.

Theft of Cars and from Cars

Unfortunately, car theft is quite common. You can expect little sympathy if your car was not locked or if the key was left in the ignition. The registration papers and your driver's license should be kept with you and not in the glove compartment, where they would be convenient for the thief but not for you when trying to recover a stolen car! Many people keep photocopies of these papers in the car.

Care should be taken regarding any possessions left in the car. If you must leave something, put it in the trunk or out of sight on the floor, even if the car is locked. If you are traveling across the country in a loaded car, try to park it where you can see it when you stop for meals. At night take all visible items with you into your motel or hotel. Put the rest in the locked trunk.

Service Stations

Cars are now made to take only unleaded gasoline. Leaded gasoline pollutes the air and can cause lead poisoning, especially in small children.

Prices vary by company and by area or state, depending on local taxes, but in general gasoline in the United States is cheaper than in most countries of the world. You can pay with cash or credit card. The U.S. gallon is approximately four liters, slightly smaller than the British imperial gallon.

At full-service stations or full-service islands, you can ask for free services, such as checking the oil and tires, and cleaning the windshield. You do not tip gas station attendants for any of these services. You can order gas by asking for a specific number of gallons, by price ("eight dollars' worth, please"), or by asking to have the tank filled up. Most tanks hold from ten to twenty gallons when full.

Most stations have self-service islands, where you put in your own gas, usually at a reduced price, and forgo other services. If your car takes diesel fuel, be sure to use diesel. Fuel pumps are designed to prevent accidentally filling a gasoline car with diesel, but not the other way around. Driving a diesel engine with gasoline will result in an unbelievably high repair bill. Even if you are relying on an attendant, be sure to remind him or her that your car takes diesel. In many gas stations, self-serve is the only option, although in a small number of states (at the time of this writing, New Jersey and Oregon), self-serve gas is not permitted and you must wait for an attendant.

If your engine is hot, do not ask the attendant to check the water in your radiator. So many attendants have been badly burned by gushing steam and water that this is no longer a regular service.

Traffic Rules

Cars travel on the right throughout the United States. By law, one must signal not only for all turns but also for lane changes. Traffic laws are being enforced more and more strictly as congestion problems grow ever more acute in American cities and on the highways. If you hear the sirens of fire trucks, ambulances, or police cars approaching, *immediately* pull over to the right and stop or slow down to let them pass.

Horn blowing is not appreciated and is prohibited in some cities; don't try to move traffic along by using your horn. You could be fined and you will surely attract the anger of other motorists.

If you come to a yellow school bus at a standstill and with flashing red lights, even if it has stopped on the opposite side of the road, you *must stop your car.* This law is strictly enforced because children may be running across the road to or from the bus.

Never stop your car on a highway. If you have a problem or want to read a map or change drivers, drive the car (or push it) well to the side of the road and switch on the emergency lights. Speeds on our highways are so fast that a stopped car is extremely dangerous, for oncoming drivers cannot see that it is stationary until they are too close to stop or swerve to avoid a collision.

Never pass on a curve or near the top of a hill; don't ever cross solid yellow or white lines, double or single. These are among the most common offenses police look for. They also watch for anyone going through a red light or a stop sign at an intersection or making a U-turn on a highway. In some states you can turn right on a red light after coming to a complete stop if you are in the outside lane; in others, you cannot. Also, some intersections are marked "no right turn on red." You can be stopped and fined for any of these faults.

Traffic lights are controlled for different speeds; in large cities these vary depending on the area, flow of traffic, and time of day. Often they are set for 25 miles per hour. If you try to find and maintain the set speed, you will "make" most lights and flow with the traffic. Talk to taxi drivers about this. They are experts at making lights and can give you many tips.

Speed Limits

Although you will see people driving at high speeds, speed limits *can* be — and often are — strictly enforced by radar, by police helicopters, by unmarked police cars, and sometimes by regular police cars that radio to one another up and down the highways.

Watch all road signs carefully as you drive along. Speed limits change frequently at various locations. *Do what they say.* They may decrease suddenly, for example, at the approach to a small town or built-up area, a factory roadway, or a railroad. They are particularly enforced in school zones, which extend on either side of any school, are clearly posted as "School Zone," and are usually posted at 15 miles per hour. It is essential to reduce speed drastically in such zones. Small children may cross the road by themselves on their way to or from school; they may also play and ride bicycles along the edge of the road and therefore create a hazard.

Parking Rules

When you park a car, read the signs carefully. Parking regulations vary in different parts of the city, at different times of the day, on different days of the week, or during different seasons of the year. The only way you can know what is legal for that particular spot is to read the sign. Many cars are towed away each day by city police for parking violations. It is not worth the risk to disobey the rules. You must pay the towing cost, expenses for actually retrieving your car, and a heavy fine for parking illegally in the first place. The whole thing can add up to several hundred dollars. In addition, you go through endless red tape, embarrassment, and inconvenience. Be careful not to park near fire hydrants, bus stops, private driveways, or too near the corner at intersections. Being towed away can result from any of these parking violations, as well as for being in a "no parking" area. In cities where it snows during the winter, signs are often posted for snow removal after a storm. Do not park on a street so posted.

The following are some common parking rules:

1. *No stopping.* This means what it says, you cannot park or even stop.

2. *No parking.* Here you may stop long enough to pick up or discharge passengers or to drop off merchandise. You can stop your car for a brief time if someone stays in the driver's seat and is able to move the car if necessary.

3. *No standing.* You may only drop people off or pick them up if you can do it quickly. You cannot wait for anyone, and you cannot leave the car while you deliver a parcel or message.

4. *Fire hydrants.* The rule is no standing or parking within 15 feet.

5. *Bus stops and taxi stands.* If you do not interfere with traffic, you can pause briefly, but you cannot get out of the car. You must be able to move at a moment's notice.

Hitchhikers

You will sometimes see people of either sex "thumbing" a ride, especially along the main highways. *Do not* stop for them. Unfortunately, this practice can be quite dangerous, as hitchhikers may not be as innocent as they look. Furthermore, in many states it is as illegal to pick up a person as it is to ask for rides. You can be fined quite heavily and lose your insurance for picking up a hitchhiker.

Finding Restrooms

A newly arrived visitor from Scotland was asked what had been the most difficult thing for him on his first day in the United States. Without a moment's hesitation, he answered, "Finding a men's room."

Some countries have public restrooms plainly visible on the street or in small buildings that are clearly marked. The United States does not. Americans find facilities in such public places as restaurants, libraries, museums, or department stores. Reasonably clean restrooms are available at most gasoline stations, but toilets at bus terminals or railroad stations may be unpleasant, and restrooms in subway stations are sometimes unsafe.

You can always go into a hotel and use the facilities, whether or not you are registered there as a guest; you will usually find them somewhere off the main lobby. Many Americans use the restrooms at national fast-food franchises, even if they are not customers. Although the restaurant owners are probably displeased by this practice, the staff rarely seem to mind. The restrooms there are usually clean and, except in very large cities, unlocked and easy to find.

Don't be confused by the name on the door. Sometimes it is marked "Men" or "Women," sometimes "Gentlemen" or "Ladies," or there may be no words used at all, just a picture of a woman or a man or some other clue painted on the door. The European designations "comfort station" or "W.C." are not used. If you are in need, just ask for the "men's room" or the "ladies' room." Some theme-based restaurants may use other languages or even puns based on their themes. One Australia-themed chain restaurant, for example, uses "blokes" for men and "sheilas" for women, and one canine-themed restaurant uses "pointers" for men and "setters" for women!

In a large hotel or restaurant, leave a tip in the small saucer if there is an attendant — 50¢ is common. One does not tip in clubs, but a smile and a friendly word are appreciated. In some public restrooms there may also be some "pay toilets," although these have been abolished by law in most states. A coin must be inserted in the door to unlock the stall so you may enter.

Part IV

For Those Who
Stay Longer

16
Housing

Finding a place to live can be one of the most challenging and stressful parts of many people's experience, especially in a new country. There are a seemingly endless number of housing options available to you, and in many parts of the country none of them are inexpensive. With careful planning and adequate information, however, you will be able to find a place to live and soon be calling it "home."

How to Begin Looking

As is generally true throughout the world, the farther you are from any urban center, the lower the rent will be. However, transportation may be so overcrowded and expensive that you will have to balance these two factors in deciding where to seek housing. Naturally, it is easier to take part in the life of a city if you live within its boundaries. For this reason single people and couples without children often prefer to live as close to the city as possible. However, families with children are generally attracted to the suburbs, where they can find larger houses at lower rents, better schools, and a slower pace — not to mention grass and trees!

If your children are of school age, the quality of local schools should be of primary concern before you decide where to rent. Many families have found that in the end it was less costly to move to a fairly expensive suburb with good public schools rather than to a less expensive neighborhood where inadequate or crowded public schools lead them to send their children to costly private schools. If there are several children in your family, this is a particularly important consideration. See Chapter 19 for a discussion of schools.

Once the school question has been explored, commuting conditions should be investigated — train or bus schedules, highways, available types of transportation, commuting time.

Your employer or foreign-student adviser should be able to give you helpful advice about schools and commuter schedules in suburban areas. You will be able to judge a good deal for yourself by driving through a number of neighborhoods. Talk to the local librarian, a salesperson, or a gas station attendant; investigate neighborhoods or suburbs as thoroughly as possible before you actually select one.

If you are moving to a medium-sized (about 500,000 population) or small city (about 100,000 population) or to a small town, the housing situation will be quite different from that in large metropolitan areas. Neighborhoods within these cities may be as spacious as those in the suburbs, although houses will sometimes be older. Public transportation, however, is frequently limited in smaller cities.

Sources of Information

Your best source of information about either houses or apartments is likely to be the local newspaper. As a rule the week's most complete real estate section appears in the Sunday edition of city newspapers. Try to get a copy on Saturday! Usually the real estate section is printed early. Timing is important, as there is often tremendous competition for housing. You need to read the columns carefully the night before so that on Sunday morning you can telephone early (even at 8 A.M.) about rentals that seem interesting to you.

There are real estate agents in all localities, and many of them handle rentals. These can be helpful, but if you can find a house yourself through friends, the newspaper, or by seeing a "For Rent" sign, it will be cheaper. Agents charge steep fees — a month's rent is common, but so is one-half month's rent. Depending on the rental market, the landlord may pay this fee or split it with you. Some companies pay such fees for their employees; others do not. Be certain you understand your company's policy regarding this matter, and inquire about fees before you sign with any real estate agency.

Even Americans are confused by the terms used in real estate advertisements. A tiny hallway, an alcove off the kitchen, or an "L" in the living room may be called a room. Sometimes kitchens and bathrooms are counted as rooms, and sometimes they are not. When you see "2-½ rooms" listed, you cannot be certain what this means. Neither can Americans! The only safe thing to do is to ask when you telephone: how many rooms are included in the apartment, and what size are they? Apartments are more expensive as you go higher in a building, unless there is no elevator. You are paying for more light and less dirt and noise from the street and sometimes for a better view. Listings are often described in terms of square feet. Simply divide by three to get a rough estimate of the size in square meters.

Renting a House or Apartment

If you rent a house, in addition to the rent, you will generally be expected to pay for gas, electricity, heat, and sometimes water and sewage. You also provide (or pay for) normal maintenance, such as grass cutting, window washing, leaf raking, and snow removal. If the house has a sidewalk, you may be responsible for having it cleared of snow within a few hours after each snowfall (usually within four daylight hours).

Furnished Apartments or Houses

The word *furnished* means different things to different people. You will normally be supplied with the essentials: stove, refrigerator, beds, chairs, sofa, tables, lamps. Minimal china and glass, flatware (often rather poor), basic kitchen supplies, curtains, and some pictures may be supplied. Sometimes, but very rarely, there is a small supply of bed, bath, and table linens and blankets.

You will need to supply your favorite kitchen utensils, some table linens or place mats, extra lamps, coat hangers, whatever electrical appliances you want — such as toasters and irons — and generally, bath and bed linens and blankets. You will certainly want to bring enough of your own things to make you feel comfortable and at home. Your own pictures, books, decorations, and the like will make it seem more like home to you.

The word *unfurnished* means different things also, but generally a stove and refrigerator are included — also towel racks, light fixtures, and other such built-in items often not included in other countries. *Partly furnished* often means only that there are some large furniture items that the previous tenant didn't bother to take.

Housing Agreements and Leases

Don't sign any agreement, normally called a "lease," until you have consulted a member of your company's personnel department, a lawyer, a real estate specialist at your bank, a well-recommended real estate agent, or an official at your university.

You should understand clearly *in advance* what the lease states about ending it or renewing it if you want to stay longer, provisions for damages, number of allowed occupants, rules about children or pets, rules that apply to subletting (i.e., renting to other parties while your own lease is in effect), painting or redecorating regulations, and hidden charges — sometimes extra ones suddenly appear for such items as a TV antenna or garbage removal. Also ask when the next rent increase will occur and what it is likely to be.

When you rent an apartment, you are normally asked for one month's "security deposit" in addition to the first and sometimes the last month's rent. The security deposit will be returned to you when you leave if there has been no major damage to the premises during your occupancy. The landlord or the landlord's agent will do the inspecting. The security deposit is an assurance to the landlord that any damage to the premises will be covered. For your own protection, you should examine the apartment carefully before you sign a lease, and get the landlord's or agent's signed (written) acknowledgment of any cracks, stains, holes, scratches, or other damages that existed before you became the tenant. Otherwise, you may be charged for preexisting damages two or three years later when you leave.

If you should move before your lease runs out, you will have to negotiate with the landlord to terminate your lease unless this provision is already written into your original lease. You may have to pay the rent until another tenant can be found, but sometimes you merely forfeit your deposits. It is best to clarify this in writing if the lease does not specify. Often, you can arrange an "early out" option in exchange for a slightly higher monthly rent.

All such matters should be discussed in advance, as mentioned above, and be sure to get professional advice before signing your name to anything. Once a contract is signed, it becomes binding. It cannot be canceled, and the terms cannot be changed without great legal difficulty. Furthermore, you will then have no opportunity for any further negotiations.

To summarize, find out the following before you sign:

1. Which services and utilities are or are not included in the rent — heat, electricity, gas, air conditioning, washing machine, clothes dryer, etc.?

2. Do you have to pay a brokerage fee (if you found the apartment through an agent)? If so, how much will it be?

3. How often will the landlord repaint the apartment, and who will pay for it?

4. Exactly how long does the lease run (they vary)?

5. What are the conditions under which you can end the lease if you leave early?

6. If you should want to sublet to someone else, can you? Under what conditions?

7. Does the landlord know the size of your family? Not all apartment houses allow children.

8. Does the landlord allow pets? Have *written* permission if you are going to keep a pet.

9. If you rent a house, who pays for lawn mowing, snow removal, etc.?

Utilities

Utilities refers to gas, electricity, heat, air conditioning, and water. Stoves (sometimes called ranges) are either gas or electric. Your heating costs may or may not be included in the rent — ask! If you have to pay, ask for the average monthly cost. Central heating systems generally burn oil or gas; in some cases, apartments or even houses may have electric heating. Be particularly careful about electric heating in climates with cold winters — you may find yourself paying six or seven hundred dollars a month, just for heat.

Modern apartment buildings are nearly always equipped with centrally operated air conditioning, which can be adjusted by the occupants of each apartment. If you live in an older house, it is likely to have window air conditioners. If there are no window units and the need is great, you can rent air conditioners on a monthly basis for the few hot months.

Most of the country operates on 110-120 volt current, 60 cycles, AC. Unless your own small appliances can be converted for U.S. current, you are well advised to leave them at home. For small items, transformers can be a nuisance. However, you can buy all kinds of appliances here at reasonable prices.

In most rented apartments and some rental houses, you will not have to pay for water or sewage. Houses are metered for water, and if you have to pay for it, the bill will arrive either monthly or quarterly. Water rates are low. In most communities, the charges for water consumption and sewage are combined. Sewage is generally a flat fee per month.

You can safely drink water from taps anywhere in the United States. Do not drink from brooks, streams, or rivers, however. Pollution is widespread. Tap water may taste unpleasant because it contains a high percentage of minerals or purifying chemicals. If you find this distasteful, you can buy bottled water in the supermarket, have filters installed, or buy an inexpensive, hand-held filtering system.

Buying a House

Nothing symbolizes the American Dream more than owning your own house. Record low mortgage interest rates and a strong housing market at this writing have combined to make buying a home worth considering, especially if you will be in the same place for more than a couple of years. Although interest rates may climb again, buying a home will still likely be a sound investment for the foreseeable future. In recent years, the values for homes have continued to appreciate, which, combined with the mortgage interest tax deduction and the money saved in rent, makes buying a home a sound investment. You can often arrange a mortgage payment that is nearly the same as a monthly rent payment would be. The downside, of course, is that you will not have the benefit of a landlord to call when something in the house breaks, as it almost certainly will. Remember, too, that a home you buy can be a house, an apartment, a condominium, a townhouse, or a co-op. In other words, just about any type of housing can be purchased rather than rented.

Real Estate Agents and Brokers

You will almost certainly want a qualified real estate agent to help you. The seller's agent will usually split his or her fee with your agent. This means that you do not pay directly for your agent's services. Nevertheless, the agent is working for you, and a good agent is more than worth the fee. The seller's agent fees (paid by the seller) average around five or six percent of the home's selling price. Your agent is paid by the other agent for bringing a qualified buyer. There is really no advantage for you to try to go through this process without an agent, unless you manage to find a home that is for sale by owner (FSBO), meaning that the seller does not have a real estate agent. FSBOs are relatively rare, and in that case you would have to forgo an agent, pay your agent's fee yourself, or negotiate the fee with the seller. As long as the seller has listed the home with an agency, she or he will be paying the full fee, regardless of whether you have an agent or not.

A real estate broker closes the deal and handles the paperwork. In some states, this is handled by lawyers, but in many, a broker will close the deal. Unless you are very familiar with real estate law, it is probably foolish to try to close a real estate transaction on your own. Real estate agents usually work exclusively with (often they work for) a particular broker, so it is a team you are selecting. The best source for your real estate team, including your mortgage broker (see below) is an enthusiastic recommendation from a friend or colleague.

Mortgages

Setting up the mortgage can also be made much simpler with the help of a professional. Mortgage brokers do not represent a particular lender but can offer a number of competing rates and plans to choose from. Some things to consider include points, adjustable or fixed rates, and the length of the loan.

Some mortgages appear lower but require "points," which are additional percentage points that are paid up front, although they can usually be included in the loan amount. Basically, points should be avoided unless they come with a significantly lower annual percentage rate. Some mortgages are fixed rate, meaning they will not vary for the entire fifteen- or thirty-year period of the mortgage. Others are adjustable rate mortgages (ARMs), which start at a much lower rate but can go up over time, to a maximum that is usually much higher than a fixed rate mortgage. ARMs make good sense if you are confident that you will be staying in the house for just a few years and then selling. They may make good sense anyway, as you can almost always refinance your house if national interest rates are low. Finally, loans are typically offered in either fifteen- or thirty-year durations, although others are possible. Remember that if you can make one extra mortgage payment per year, your loan time can usually be cut about in half.

Moving In

If you've shipped your belongings from home, you must be present to receive them. As the movers unpack, check to see that each item has arrived in good condition. The person in charge of the moving crew should make a written note of any damage before you sign the bill. Once you sign it, he or she will make no further changes. If some goods are damaged, immediately obtain a claim form from the moving company (or its insurance agent). Fill out the form, make a photocopy for yourself, and then return the original promptly. Time is important. Don't delay. Also inform your employer so that their transportation specialist can advise you. If you are not reimbursed within two or three weeks, let the transportation officer of your company follow up on your claim, or do it yourself. Don't let too much time go by.

Photocopies should always be made of whatever papers, letters, claims, or counterclaims pass between you and the movers and/or the insurance company. This is very important. If your company does not make the copies for you, take the papers to a public copying machine. You will find them in post offices, banks, stationery shops, libraries, and even some stores. Having everything in detail and in the proper sequence in your files makes following up on any claim far easier and quicker.

Consult with your company some days before the movers are to arrive so that you know exactly what you can expect. Services vary widely according to the contract. Some will place your furniture, set up beds, and unpack china, silver, glassware, linens, and books. They are required to remove all packing debris. Some movers will connect your electrical appliances for you; most will not. Some will set up only large items and will not unpack small ones. Be sure to ask in advance.

Most people tip the moving crew in relation to the size and length of the job. Tips range from $5 per person for a small job up to about $20 per person for a full day's job. It is also a good idea to have cold soft drinks and coffee available if possible. This is a tiring job, so be kind to the movers and try to stay out of their way. Remember that time is money for them.

Be sure to keep track of what they are delivering in case something is missing. It can be difficult to file a claim after you have signed the paperwork saying that everything has been delivered.

17

Shopping: Getting the Most for Your Money

It might be said that shopping, rather than baseball, is the real national sport of the United States. As Paco Underhill observed, "We use shopping as therapy, reward, bribery, pastime, an excuse to get out of the house, as a way to troll for potential loved ones, as entertainment, as a form of education or even worship, as a way to kill time."[1] In the small town of Freeport, Maine, just up the road from our publisher, there are 158 stores. One of them, the flagship store of the venerable catalogue company L.L. Bean, is open 365 days a year — 24 hours a day! Should you find yourself in need of a fishing pole and complete line of tackle at 3:00 A.M. on Christmas morning, the people at L.L. Bean can help. In another small town, Bloomington, Minnesota, there is a shopping mall so large that it boasts 525 stores and claims 42 million visitors a year. Apparently that's more than the Statue of Liberty, the Empire State Building, or the Washington Monument, because the Mall of America, as it is called, asserts that it is the most visited attraction in the United States. More than 1,500 couples have been married in the Mall of America since it opened in 1992.

One newcomer to the United States, when asked his first impression, replied, "So many things to buy." And there are! You will find yourself being urged from every page of every newspaper and magazine, on the Internet, and on every TV and radio station to buy all manner of goods, which, in fact, you will be quite happy without. This constant barrage of advertising, with its emphasis on owning this or that in order to be happy, healthy, or more attractive, has given the United States the reputation of being very materialistic. It is true; this is an affluent and, therefore, materialistic nation. It is interesting to note, however, that as soon as any country grows more affluent, it tends to grow increasingly materialistic. Traffic jams develop in country after country as more people are able to buy cars; salespeople work hard in most of the world to sell televisions, watches, furniture, food, clothes, computers, or washing machines.

People everywhere seem to be alike in this respect. As soon as there is any extra money, we seek to raise and *keep on raising* our standard of living. You may not be surprised by this, but look at the bigger picture: What do people do with their new prosperity? Does it enrich their relationships with other people? How creative are they? How hard do they work? How do they spend their money?

Because so much in the United States is mass-produced, and much of it imported from countries with cheap labor, there is a large quantity of relatively inexpensive goods available to everyone. You will find a tremendous range in price, based on quality, style, area of the country, and other factors. Comparative shopping is a good idea before you buy any major item. From all of the choices available, how are you, the new arrival, going to know what to buy and how to get your money's worth? In the first place, don't hurry. Take time to look over the various kinds of stores and examine the quality of their merchandise; read the ads carefully so that you can compare prices; touch, explore, and examine before you buy, and talk to your new colleagues at work or school and ask them for recommendations. In addition, some helpful guidelines are provided below.

Food

Supermarkets in the United States keep getting bigger, and they are always confusing. How can you decide what to buy amid an amazing choice of items? Understanding some general patterns of packaging and pricing can help you evaluate the options available to you.

Price

You can save a good deal of money if you watch for sales instead of buying the same "brand-name" (a well-known company name) items at regular prices. Many supermarkets have their own label, and these items are almost always less expensive than brand-name items. You'll have to experiment, because some brand-name items are indeed tastier or better quality than less well-known brands.

Look to see if both brands contain the same number of ounces, and look at the list of ingredients to see what percentage is water. By law, actual ingredients must always be listed *in order of the amount contained.* Using "unit pricing" can also help. If, for example, you are shopping for laundry powder, the unit price will reflect how much you pay per pound. The "per pound" or "per fluid ounce" or the "per quart" prices are more important than the actual cost of an item. Large is not always less expensive.

Food Labels

The U.S. grading system for meat has nothing to do with nutrition, only with federal standards of quality for tenderness, juiciness, and flavor. The most common grades of meat are prime and choice.

Foods are marked using three categories: nutrition information per serving — calories, protein, carbohydrates, cholesterol, fat, and sodium; percentage of U.S. recommended daily allowances of these items plus vitamins and minerals; and the ingredients. It is important to know the size of a serving if you are interested in watching your weight or must eat carefully because of medical conditions such as diabetes or heart problems. Many products also have directions for preparation and suggestions for use.

Warnings

Although an increasing effort is being made to protect the buyer, there are still, unfortunately, a number of "shortcuts" or hidden factors that one needs to watch out for — sizes and weights, for example. A bottle that looks like a quart (or liter) does not necessarily contain that amount. In small print on the label, it may say "contains 24 fluid ounces" (a quart is 32 ounces). Packages meant to look like one pound may actually contain only 14 or 11 or 9 ounces worth of food. By law, weight must be printed on all food packages, under "net contents," so one can always check this, but too many of us do not take the time and trouble. Often the print is very small — on purpose!

Don't be overly concerned about these matters. You will gradually learn by experience and by trial and error, but you can shorten your learning time if you read labels and compare as you shop. You will soon find the foods your family likes and which brands are best for you. Such care and study can save you a considerable amount of money on your food bills.

The U.S. Department of Agriculture claims that those who watch carefully and who follow the weekly specials offered in all supermarkets can save about 6 percent per week.

If you have clipped a discount coupon from the newspaper and you find the same item on sale in the store, you save even more. And some supermarkets offer "double coupon" savings, meaning you save twice the amount noted on the coupon.

Any large bookstore will have a selection of books that are helpful as guides to shopping.

Returning Merchandise

If you have bought something and want to return it, you can do so with most items from nearly all department stores and often, but not always, from smaller shops. However, you *must* have the sales slip. Some stores will take returns without the receipt, but they will only refund the lowest amount the item has sold for. Thus, if it has gone on sale since you bought it, you may get back only a fraction of what you paid. So do not throw away any receipts until you are sure you are satisfied with the item.

Sometimes during a sale, the store will post a notice warning customers "All sales are final," which means that you may *not* return the item for exchange or for your money back.

If you are returning a gift that has been mailed to you from the store and therefore you have no sales receipt, save the gift slip that accompanies the item and/or take off the delivery label from the front of the package. It has various markings on it that have meaning for the clerk. If you have no label, then ask to exchange for some item of equal worth. It is often easier to do this than to get a cash refund.

Warranties

When you buy new electrical appliances, radios, TVs, or other major items such as stoves, you will probably be given some papers with them. One of these is likely to be a written warranty. This means that if anything goes wrong, you can have the item repaired free of charge for a certain length of time — for some items as long as three to five years. You should read the warranty carefully. It probably asks you to send in a postcard to establish the date of purchase. If so, be sure to do it as soon as possible. In addition, write the date of purchase on the warranty itself, along with the serial number on the appliance. Keep it somewhere safe so you can find it if you need it. The warranty will be of help *only* if you have saved the papers and complied with the instructions. You may be able to buy an extended (longer) service warranty for larger appliances for an additional fee, often up to 25 percent of the purchase price. With the drop in prices of many consumer electronics, you must weigh carefully the cost of such a warranty. With computers, digital cameras, video recorders, and so on, you can be virtually assured that in six months time, you will be able to buy a better model for less money.

Repairs

If you do not have a warranty and have problems with vacuum cleaners, toasters, radios, and so on, look under "Electric Appliances — Repairs" or "Radio (Vacuum Cleaner, etc.) Repair" in the Yellow Pages of the telephone book. Try to find a repair shop specializing in your particular brand name, if possible. Other kinds of repairs — china, glass, zippers, etc. — are also listed by item in most phone books. Repairs are very expensive, however, and you may be charged a minimum fee just to have the item examined, particularly if you ask someone to come to your home to repair a large piece of equipment or an appliance. Sadly, in most cases involving small appliances, it is cheaper to replace an item than to repair it.

Telephone Sales

If anyone tries to sell you an item over the telephone, just say "No, thank you" and hang up without any further conversation. Credit cards, long-distance telephone services, magazines — all sorts of things — may be offered. Don't get involved! They may try to tempt you with every kind of prize, free demonstration, or gift. Most reputable firms do not use this technique for selling (although a few do), nor do they use door-to-door salespeople — but newcomers to the United States should take no chances with telephone sales. It is foolhardy to do so. In fact, as of 2003, you can request that your telephone number be registered in the national "do-not-call" list (www.donotcall.gov/). Telemarketers who call numbers on this list are subject to a penalty of $500, payable to the victim. This can be filed in small claims court.

Installment Plans

Generally speaking, avoid buying on the installment plan — paying part of the cost when you obtain a product or service and the rest in installments, most often monthly. Interest and fees are high and often hidden in the fine print. Once you have signed the agreement, you are obligated to make the payments. There is no way out, so tread carefully. Mortgages on real estate, financing on the purchase of a car, or similar loans on very large purchases may be necessary, but try to avoid burdening yourself with monthly payments on such luxury items as TVs, stereos, dishwashers, or tempting trips to sunny beaches in the Caribbean. You often pay one-third or one-half as much again as the regular price by the time all fees and interest costs have been added. Buying by credit card and paying only part of your bill each month is essentially the same as installment buying. Although credit cards have the virtue of simplicity, you are running up extra charges if you don't pay off the complete balance monthly.

Comparison Shopping and Reduced Prices

Americans do not usually bargain over prices, as people do in much of the world. What they do instead is shop around to find the store that offers the item and quality they want at the lowest price. Almost everything sold in the United States varies in price according to the store and often the time of year (just before Christmas is often highest; lowest is just after Christmas or during August, when many stores have sales). Sales accompany most national holidays, such as President's Day, Memorial Day, and Labor Day. The day after Thanksgiving and the day after Christmas are also significant sales days. Sale prices are often indicated by a sign over the merchandise rather than a change on the price tag of each item. Make sure that you are actually charged the sale price; inaccurate computers are not uncommon. The sale price may be a percentage off the regular price or listed as a dollar amount.

Sometimes the price varies according to state or local taxes. Many people cross state lines to buy liquor, cigarettes, or electronics, for example, because there are wide fluctuations in taxes on such items from state to state.

If it is important to you to save money, look for the discount stores in your city. They exist all across the country and are growing in popularity. Much of what they sell is comparable to goods sold elsewhere, but they can offer lower prices for any one or all of these reasons: there may be fewer salespeople (less service); often there is no delivery service except for heavy items like refrigerators; floor space is often so fully used that the store is congested; the decor is simple to save the cost of fancy carpeting or expensive interiors; or goods may be sold only in bulk, that is, in large containers or large quantities and stacked to the ceiling as in a warehouse. These discount stores may be electronics stores (e.g., Circuit City); clothing stores (e.g., Marshall's and Ross Dress for Less); huge hardware and home decorating and repair stores (e.g., Home Depot, Home Base, Lowes,); office supply stores (e.g., Office Max, Staples, Office Depot); and department stores that sell almost everything (e.g., Wal-Mart, Kmart, Target).

In some of these stores you pay a membership fee (e.g., Price Club, Costco, and Sam's Club). Because they are so colorful and have such a variety of goods, these discount stores are often of interest to newcomers who find that wandering through them helps in learning American names for unfamiliar items. There are also liquidation stores such as Building 19, Big Lots, Odd Lots, and Dollar Stores that sell high quality but discontinued household items for extremely low prices.

In most discount houses you will find clothing hanging on long racks. Shoes, socks, or underwear may be piled up in bins. It is advisable to look for those items that carry familiar brand names as much as possible, or ask a neighbor or friend to go with you. Although some of these goods are the very same that you would buy in other stores at higher prices, often they are made with inferior materials and poorly assembled.

Buying Secondhand

So many people are constantly on the move in the United States that it is easy to find secondhand household goods for sale. Buying secondhand is quite usual here. Many young couples furnish new homes this way. People who do not want to spend time or a lot of money shopping sometimes buy the entire furnishings of an apartment from someone who is moving to another part of the country.

Many communities have a weekly bulletin that contains nothing but classified advertisements. If you look there or in the local daily and weekly newspapers, you will see advertisements in the classified section that read, for example:

"Moving, entire contents of house for sale."

"Going to California; desk, large clock, child's bicycle for sale."

"Redecorating house, complete maple living room furniture for sale."

"Dining room set for sale."

"Queen sized bed, good condition, with almost-new mattress for sale."

If you see something that interests you, call *at once* on the telephone; some things are often sold very quickly. If the item is still available, go immediately to examine it. If you like it, you can try bargaining. Then you must work out a means of getting your purchase (or purchases) to your house. This can be a major problem, but the easiest solution (if you have no friend with a pickup truck or van) is to look at ads in the local paper or in the Yellow Pages under "Trucking" or "Hauling" to find someone with a truck. Otherwise, rent a van, truck, or trailer (to attach to your car) from Ryder, U-Haul, or another rental company. Give a deposit to hold the goods and *get a receipt.* Don't pay the full price until you come back to pick up the item(s). Most people are honest, but some are not — so you need to be careful.

Auctions, Garage Sales, and Yard Sales

Garage or yard sales are very popular. People collect all the items they no longer need or want, such as furniture, glassware, china, clothing, books, toys, and so forth, and hold a one- or two-day sale in their garage or yard. Sometimes several families or even an entire neighborhood will hold a cooperative sale. Although many yard or garage sales are advertised in local newspapers, smaller sales may just be announced by signs on the streets near the sale site. Many people drive around on Saturday mornings hunting for these sales. Good bargains can often be found, and talking with the owners and other customers is fun.

Buying in this way is a good deal more trouble than buying new equipment from a store and having it delivered, but it can also be much cheaper. Many times you get real bargains and high quality, especially if the owners must move and are in a hurry to dispose of their goods, or if, as is often the case with an auction, someone has died and an estate is being settled.

Thrift Shops

Thrift shops are run by charities (such as Goodwill or the Salvation Army) that first collect and then sell used clothes, sports equipment, books, china, glassware, furniture, and so on. The charities then donate the money they collect to some particular school, hospital, nursing home, or other institution.

There is no loss of face in buying at thrift shops. Many middle- or upper-class people donate to them, help run them, and also buy from them. They are particularly good for such items as children's clothes (often outgrown before they were much used) or evening dresses, which the well-to-do donate after a few wearings, and which most of us wear so seldom that we want to buy at minimum cost. Many people go to thrift shops for ice skates, tennis rackets, books, pictures, lamps, or extra items for their new homes. By law, all clothing given to reputable shops has been washed or dry-cleaned and inspected.

A relatively new type of thrift store is the secondhand consignment store, usually specializing in women's (and sometimes children's) clothing, shoes, and accessories. The seller receives a percentage of the sale of her items — if they sell, that is.

Internet, Catalogue, and TV Sales

One of the largest retail operations in the United States is selling by mail through catalogues and through the Internet. Catalogues will arrive in your mail on a regular basis, and you can purchase anything from gourmet food to fur coats by mail, phone, or via the Internet. Growth in this sector has occurred for several reasons. People have less time for shopping — especially in two-career families — and retailers can reach a greater number of people. Most important is that shopping by mail is convenient, especially for the elderly or others who cannot move around easily. The disadvantage, of course, is that you cannot try on clothes or examine the products. Most companies who sell this way are very reputable and readily accept returns if you are not satisfied with the merchandise. Don't be surprised if you receive catalogues from companies you have never purchased from; many catalogue companies make extra money by selling their mailing list to other firms.

Auction sites on the Internet, such as eBay, are a popular form of shopping for both new and used goods. You may be amazed at the variety of goods being sold by auction, and if you take some time to educate yourself about market value, you can get some good deals. You can check to see what items similar to the one you want have recently sold for and check the feedback other buyers have given to various sellers. Amazon.com is an enormous Internet retail site. You can buy books, clothing, toys and games, DVDs, and much more. As always, buyer beware.

In recent years, a number of televisions shows — and even entire 24-hour channels — have sprung up, aimed at the television viewer. These shows feature items at supposedly discounted prices, though you may frequently be able to find comparable prices in local stores. They display a variety of merchandise from clothing, jewelry, clocks, luggage, and toys to small kitchen gadgets, hardware, and exercise equipment.

To order from one of these TV vendors, you select the item you want, phone in your order, paying by either credit card, money order, or check, and wait for your selection to be shipped to you.

A word of caution: many people impulsively order items from these shows that they neither want nor need — and cannot afford. It is all too easy to get carried away by TV salespeople urging you to call in immediately to take advantage of this "limited-time" offer. Take care to avoid this situation. Also, quality varies tremendously among these products.

18
Household Help and Care of Young Children

L
ive-in, domestic help is prohibitively expensive nowadays for all but the wealthiest Americans. More common forms of domestic help are (1) cleaning women, who come in once or twice a week or even every two weeks, and (2) baby-sitters, who stay with children when the parents go out. Otherwise, precooked and packaged foods, microwave ovens, no-iron fabrics, dishwashers, and washing machines — all time- and labor-saving devices — take the place of household help.

Household Cleaning or Party Help

The best way to find someone to clean your house is by asking people you know for recommendations. Start with your friends or your business acquaintances. This is a common request, and you need not feel embarrassed. Americans are accustomed to helping each other find domestic help, just as they are to recommending a doctor or dentist. People will ask their own domestic help if they have extra time, or if they know a relative or a friend who might be looking for work.

You can also ask the manager or superintendent of your apartment house. Perhaps there is someone already working in the building who wants more work. Sometimes the clerks at local laundries, grocery stores, pharmacies, or the like can give you suggestions. If you are known to be a regular customer, such people are likely to recommend people carefully.

If you cannot find anyone by word of mouth, there are other methods, though these tend to be less satisfactory. You can use a maid service, for example, listed in the Yellow Pages. Such services are more expensive; on the other hand, they assume responsibility for troublesome details like Social Security payments, insurance, and so on. There are also companies that offer housecleaning services. They send a team of well-equipped people in to clean your house on a weekly, biweekly, or monthly schedule, and to wash windows, clean rugs, and do similar heavy work at regular intervals — or once or twice a year, as you request. Housecleaning help is a growing industry in the United States, generally providing excellent services.

Another option is an employment agency, although it is likely to be expensive and is not preferred. There is no guarantee that the person will stay with you beyond the period covered by the usually high agency fee. Furthermore, you may have to interview many people. If you use this method, be sure to ask for references, both for the candidate and for the agency. Not every agency is dependable.

You can also advertise in the newspaper for a housecleaner. The difficulty with this method is that you know nothing about the people who may come to your house to be interviewed. If you do follow this method, check each reference very carefully before hiring, and don't try it unless your English is very good.

Finally, you can answer an advertisement. People who are looking for work frequently advertise their services. This way of finding help is particularly useful in smaller towns and rural areas where it is easier to find out about your potential employee. In larger towns and cities, be sure to interview carefully and check references thoroughly. Some of the best prospects are found in foreign language newspapers.

Many small catering companies specialize in residential parties. They may bring in food that has been prepared elsewhere or use your kitchen to do the preparation. You can ask the caterer to provide all the help your event needs, or you can limit it as you see fit and negotiate. If you go to a party you enjoy, ask the hosts if they hired a caterer or other help and for suggestions for your party. People are usually happy to make recommendations. You can also hire waitresses, cooks, bartenders, or butlers by the hour.

If you live in a town with a college or university, call its employment bureau. Some colleges hold extracurricular training programs in household skills or bartending to help students get jobs.

Childcare

American adults move around a great deal and often live far away from their parents. Because they have established their own homes and developed their own lifestyles, their children do not grow up surrounded by grandparents, aunts, uncles, and cousins, as children do in many cultures. Most families have only one, two, or three children close together in age, so there is rarely one child old enough to look after the others. These facts, along with the reality that in modern American families single-parent and dual-career parents are common, have made childcare a vital part of the American scene.

Baby-sitters

A "sitter" is someone who is hired to care for children for a specific length of time — usually relatively short — while the parents are out for the evening attending a party or taking a class, for example. Sometimes the baby-sitter is also hired for longer periods, perhaps when the parents are away for a weekend. In such cases the sitter is likely to be a mature and motherly woman. For a short period, teenagers, college students, and others (of either sex) are commonly employed on an hourly basis.

From the point of view of convenience, the best sitters are often young people who live in your apartment building or close by in the neighborhood. This gives you a chance to meet the parents and interview the sitter. If an emergency occurs, young sitters can call upon their parents quickly for help. Another advantage is that you do not have to take them far to see them home at night or pay expensive taxi fares. Finally, young people living close by can usually fill in quite readily on short notice or for short periods of time.

In an apartment house you can ask the superintendent for permission to post a notice for a baby-sitter by the mailboxes. This is often the best way to find out if there is anyone in the building who is interested in baby-sitting. Retired people as well as students are often glad to earn a little money in this way.

An excellent source for baby-sitters is a nearby college or university. Students frequently want to earn extra money in their spare time. The best procedure is to go to the school before you need a sitter and ask if you can post an advertisement on bulletin boards or put an ad in the student-run newspaper. With any luck, you might find one or two students who speak your own language.

The disadvantage of using students is that they are often busy in the evenings, they are gone during their holidays, and sometimes they bring along their friends. The advantage is that they are less expensive than anyone from an agency and, being young, are likely to be more fun for your children.

Other sources could be the bulletin board of the local YWCA or the Girl Scouts, who sometimes organize baby-sitting services. Some scout troops train older girls, who earn service credits in this way. They are a particularly good possibility if you want someone to remain indoors and play with the children. Since they are young themselves, you might not want to give them outside responsibility such as taking children through traffic.

As you make friends, don't hesitate to ask if their teenagers would like to baby-sit. Often they are delighted. Baby-sitting is a popular occupation for teenagers, especially girls, so do not be shy about asking them whether or not they are available. Most mothers try to line up three or four sitters whom they (and the children) get to know and like. In this way they have alternate numbers to call when their favorite baby-sitter is not available.

A young couple with children, struggling along on a tight budget — especially students — often work out an exchange agreement with another couple, sitting for each other's children a certain number of hours or evenings a week. The mothers exchange daytime hours as well, giving each other occasional or regular free afternoons for shopping, working part-time, taking classes, going to the hairdresser, or visiting friends.

Rates vary widely by location and age — less money for teenagers than for mature women, for example. You pay more for daytime hours than the period after children are in bed until midnight. After that, rates may go up again. You pay more, of course, if you have several children or if the job includes preparing a meal. Many sitters don't want to cook and you should not expect it, although feeding the children meals that you have prepared is normally acceptable.

If you have a small baby and want someone older and more experienced than a student, look under "Nannies" or "Baby-sitting Services" in the Yellow Pages. If you employ the same person regularly for even a few hours per month, you must pay Social Security taxes (see below) unless you get her through an agency. In that case the agency will do the paperwork for you.

Day-Care Centers

Day-care centers range from a stay-at-home mom (or dad!) who take in a small number of other children during the day to make extra money, to large commercial enterprises. Many states license day-care centers, and it is best to become familiar with the licensing criteria in your state so you know what it entails. Unfortunately, in many cases, licensure is only a bare minimum of declarations by the provider, so do not infer that a licensed center has been inspected or its staff evaluated. There are also private associations that have higher standards, and accredit centers that meet those standards. The National Association for the Education of Young Children (www.naeyc.org/), the Network of Child Care Resource and Referral (www.nccrra.org/), and Child Care Aware (www.childcareware.org/) are all excellent resources. Your employer and coworkers may also have suggestions. In the end, personal referrals of satisfied parents may be the most reliable way to choose. Many religious institutions run day-care centers during the week, as do YMCAs and YWCAs. Parents need not be members to enroll their children. Some list members who like to baby-sit; some have set up group baby-sitting for certain afternoons during the week so that mothers can shop or attend to other necessities. Most religious institutions also have nurseries and baby-sitting services on Sunday (or Saturday) mornings so that parents can attend services. There is usually no charge — or only a nominal one — for this service.

Public or private day-care centers and neighborhood centers are another good resource in your community. They may be advertised in the local newspaper, but there is such a shortage of good day-care centers that frequently one must learn of them by asking neighbors and acquaintances. It may be necessary to put your child on a waiting list, so it is never too early to inquire. A note of warning: never choose a daycare center or nursery school without checking it out carefully *and* obtaining references or personal recommendations from friends or colleagues.

Taxes on Household Employees

Household employees include workers such as cooks, cleaning people, baby-sitters, handymen, drivers, and gardeners. Under certain circumstances you are required to pay Social Security taxes for those employees on a percentage of the total wages paid. This amount may be matched by the employee, or you may pay the whole amount. You, the employer, are responsible for mailing the total amount of tax to your local Internal Revenue Service (IRS) office within thirty days after the end of each calendar quarter. Once you have paid your first tax, the IRS will send you a quarterly reminder. There is a penalty if you do not pay the tax on time. The amounts involved are not great, even when you pay the full tax yourself.

You should consult a tax preparer, such as a certified public accountant (CPA), to find out what your obligation is regarding these taxes. Also, you can telephone the nearest office of the IRS and ask for the proper instructions and forms for filing this tax. If your friends or neighbors employ household workers, you can ask them how they handle this matter.

19

Educating Your Children

Education is an important part of American life, and the wide variety of educational choices is sometimes difficult for visitors from other countries to understand. One-half of all the people in the country between the ages of 18 and 25 are enrolled in a college, university, or technical training institute. All boys and girls up to age 16 are required to go to school. There are three broad categories of education that serve this population: (1) public schools (including charter, magnet, and vocational schools), (2) private schools (including religious, boarding, day, Montessori, and Waldorf schools), and (3) home schooling.

Education here is intended for everyone. Schools are expected to meet the needs of every child, regardless of ability, and also the needs of society itself. This means that tax-supported public schools offer more than academic subjects. It surprises many people when they come here to find high schools offering such courses as typing, sewing, radio repair, computer programming, or driver training along with traditional academic subjects such as mathematics, history, and languages. Students choose from a large selection of courses, depending on state requirements, their interests, future goals, and level of ability. The underlying goal of American education is to develop every child to the utmost of his or her abilities and to give each one a sense of civic and community consciousness.

Because our population is so diverse, schools have traditionally played an important role in creating national unity and in "Americanizing" the millions of immigrants who have poured into this country. Schools also play an important role in the community, especially in small towns.

The American approach to teaching may seem unfamiliar to many, not only because it is informal, but also because there is less emphasis on learning facts than is true in the systems of many other countries. Instead, Americans try to teach their children to think for themselves, to analyze, to explore, to develop their own intellectual and creative abilities. Students spend much time learning how to use resource materials, libraries, and computers. Americans believe that if children are taught to reason and to research well, they will be able to find whatever facts they need throughout the rest of their lives. Knowing how to solve problems is considered more important than the accumulation of facts, which often grow obsolete.

Computers are used in many classrooms, frequently starting in kindergarten. If your child does not know how to use a computer, you can help him or her a great deal by providing computer lessons in advance, even while you are still in your own country. To find such classes after you arrive in the United States, consult the school or ask a local computer store where classes are given.

Naturally, when any family moves from one country to another, the question of schooling for their children is always an urgent one. Unless you are in a small town, there will be a variety of schools — public, parochial, or private; day or boarding; coeducational or all-boy/all-girl; traditional or experimental — available to you.

The School Year

In most areas the school year begins in late August or early September and ends somewhere near the middle or end of June. A few schools, generally at the high school level, also offer summer sessions. These are optional, but they give students a chance to make up work that they have missed or failed, take advance credits or extra courses they have not had time for in the school year, or just become familiar with a school before the new term starts. Summer sessions normally hold classes in the morning and then offer a range of sports, trips, and leisure activities in the afternoon.

If you arrive in the United States in the spring with a teenager who plans to enter a regular school session in September, you might want to consider enrolling him or her in summer courses to improve English language proficiency, make friends, or gain self-confidence. A new and interesting trend is starting among some schools, particularly on the west coast, namely a shift to a year-long pattern rather than having long summer holidays.

Nursery Schools and Preschools

There is such variation in preschools and nursery schools that it is best to wait until you arrive to see what is available in your neighborhood. Private nursery schools are often expensive, but there are also informal play groups, religious-affiliated nursery schools, YMCAs, YWCAs, or other less expensive possibilities in most communities.

Little children often attend these for only three to four hours, two or three days a week, but they start to learn about sharing, following instructions, and being part of a group. They also enjoy the companionship of other children their age, which is often hard to find in city living.

If you live in an area where there are many small children and an outdoor place to play, you probably will not need such an organized group. However, in impersonal apartment houses, children are sometimes lonely. In addition, you may want to give your children a little extra help in learning American ways and English before they start school, which can be a rough adjustment.

If you do not find a preschool that you like near your home, you may find that there are dance classes, art classes, gymnastics classes, swimming lessons, or other activities for little children, where you can bring your child into contact with playmates once or twice a week.

Large apartment units often provide day care or supervised play groups for little children during certain hours of the week. Mothers sometimes pool their resources and take turns with each other's children, partly to give themselves an occasional free afternoon and partly to give their children needed companionship. See the section on "Day-Care Centers" in Chapter 18 for help in selecting a nursery school or preschool.

Public Schools

The great majority of American children attend public schools, that is, schools that are tax-supported and free. It is often confusing to newcomers to find that there is no national standardized system for all fifty states. Each state has been free to develop its own model. These vary so widely in quality, facilities, disciplines, and academic standards that people often move in to (or out of) a state because of the quality of available schooling.

To make matters even more confusing, local school districts have considerable decision-making authority *within* each state framework. City, township, and district schools have their own curricula, boards, budgets, and standards, even though these must follow certain broad guidelines outlined by their states.

School support comes primarily from taxes at state and local levels, rather than from national funds. When the federal government does contribute to education, it does so primarily in the poorer states, where local funds are inadequate. National funds tend to be channeled for buildings, transportation, or other projects that do not affect the curriculum. As previously noted, Americans jealously guard their independence from their own national government. If there is a chance that, as a result of accepting national funds, the government may be able to exert some kind of control, such funds are often turned down by community school boards (elected citizens). There have been heated arguments — even riots and demonstrations at the college level — when citizens have felt that the federal government was exerting too strong an influence on curriculum through support of scientific research programs, for example, or military training, or other specific projects. Since many of our ancestors and many of today's new citizens have come to this country for the express purpose of escaping too much government control, this feeling still runs deep.

In line with this emphasis on local control over education, there are no national examinations at either school or college level as there are, for example, in France, England, or Japan. College Board examinations, which are taken across the country for entrance to colleges and universities, are administered by a private organization, not by the federal government, and no college is compelled to use them. This state and local independence results in substantial variation in the quality of public education, even from one town to the next. In our fast-growing cities, elementary and high schools are nearly all badly overcrowded. In recent years many have been troubled with violence, teacher strikes, and other problems. In suburban areas and small towns, public schools tend to be more settled, with adequate facilities, reasonable ratios between teachers and pupils, and good academic standards.

The pendulum (between state and federal control on one side and local control on the other) does swing, however. There is a national law that requires school districts to implement standardized tests and it requires them all to use the same test. Several states have had a standardized testing program for a number of years.

As a newcomer, you may raise questions and talk as freely as you like about schooling with any Americans you meet. Many people here are deeply concerned about education. They constantly discuss the subject among themselves, and they will be delighted to talk with you about it also. Much is good and much is bad in our current educational establishment. We are in the process of reevaluating and restructuring the whole educational system of this country in order to meet our current needs and the urgent needs of the twenty-first century, including many new pressures from our vast and rapidly changing population.

Vocational Schools

Many school districts offer a distinct curriculum for those students who are not preparing to go on to higher education. In the last two years of high school, they may take courses in cosmetology, automobile or computer repair, or other fields. Vocational schools are aimed at moving their graduates quickly into skilled and semiskilled occupations. Because nearly half the eighteen-year-olds do not attend college or university, vocational education is an important part of the educational system.

Magnet Schools

Many school districts offer schools with specialized curricula, such as an emphasis on arts, science, or foreign languages. Students are admitted to the programs competitively, and unlike other public schools, enrollment is not assigned by the student's address. If your city or school district offers magnet schools, it is worth the effort to learn more about them. Magnet Schools of America (www.magnet.edu/) is a good place to start.

Charter Schools

Somewhere between public and private schools are charter schools, so called because they receive a charter from the state in order to operate. These are publicly funded, privately operated schools that receive extremely high levels of autonomy from state or local regulations governing public schools. In the 1990s, there was a dramatic increase in charter schools, especially in large cities. These schools are funded based on the number of students they enroll. Freed from the burdens of teacher unions and the obligation to educate every student, charter schools evoke heated passions from both supporters and detractors. On the one hand, they generally provide a superior education and attract the brightest and most capable students. On the other hand, they drain limited funding from the larger urban schools, as well as leaving behind those who are most difficult to teach. Some of these schools have curricular emphases such as science or foreign languages. Charter schools offer many of the benefits of private schools without charging high tuition. You can find more information at www.uscharterschools.org/.

Private and Parochial Schools

An extensive network of private schools parallels the public school system. Some of these schools are closely associated with a church or religious denomination and are called parochial schools. Some of these, such as those sponsored by the Society of Friends (Quakers) and many Catholic schools, are popular among people of all faiths. Private schools receive no financial support from tax funds and are, with the exception of some parochial schools, expensive — some more so than others.

Why do people spend so much money, often to the point of major financial sacrifice, to send their children to private schools? The reasons vary.

1. Classes tend to be smaller with greater individual attention than in public schools. Some children need this kind of supportive individual instruction.

2. Most private schools are highly selective; through interviews, references, and examinations (at least for the upper levels), they seek students of quality. This means that they can usually maintain higher

academic standards than the public schools, which have to accept students of all abilities.

3. Discipline is likely to be better and academic standards higher than in public schools, which are often overcrowded and understaffed.

4. Some parents living in crowded or academically disadvantaged areas feel they must send their children to private schools to prepare them for admission to a selective college.

5. A few parents prefer to send their children to schools sponsored by their own religious denomination.

6. Some parents seek a more homogeneous student body than is found in the public schools.

Those interested in finding out about private schools can contact the National Association of Independent Schools at www.nais.org/.

Boarding schools exist mostly for children of high school age (15–18), though there are also a few for younger children. If you happen to settle near a boarding school, you may be able to enroll your child as a day student. Otherwise, these children live in school dormitories and attend classes on the school campus.

You may find private schools teaching in German, Spanish or French, or adhering to a specific educational philosophy such as Montessori or Waldorf. Contact the Council for American Private Education (www.capenet.org/) for more information.

Relationships between Parents and School

Most schools have organizations made up of both parents and teachers. They meet together regularly to discuss and confer on various matters pertaining to the school — curriculum, budgets, faculty, salaries, library facilities, and so forth.

Parents often volunteer to help with classroom or after-school activities. They sometimes make costumes for plays, play the piano, bring snacks or cookies for a party, or assist a teacher on a class field trip. Some come at regular times to tutor children in the classroom, under the teacher's supervision. Volunteering at your child's school is a good way to meet people in the area and to learn how the school functions.

In good schools a real effort is made to have the home and the school work together for the child's well-being. You will generally find teachers eager to talk with you about any problems you may have concerning your child — although the larger the class, the less time (understandably) the teachers have. Where size permits, there are often parent conferences — scheduled appointments so that parents can meet privately with one or more of their child's teachers to discuss particular problems or progress. You will also be sent notices of meetings or programs. You may be invited to a "parents' day," where you follow your child's schedule through a full day of classes, or a "parents' evening," an abbreviated version, with ten- to fifteen-minute classes. This is enlightening and enjoyable for most parents. Parent-teacher conferences may be scheduled regularly or at the request of either the teacher or the parents. These conferences are an important way to understand what is expected of your child, and to find out whether he or she is experiencing any academic or social difficulties.

Both mothers and fathers are expected to attend such meetings and to show their interest in the school and their children's education. School functions also provide a good way to meet your neighbors and to make friends in the community. Since Americans enjoy meeting people from other countries, you will probably find your national background a help rather than a handicap in getting acquainted. This is true even if you are having trouble with the language.

After-School or Extracurricular Activities

American children are among the most scheduled in the world. In addition to their academic work, children in the United States are offered a wide range of activities sponsored by the school during after-school hours. These activities, usually called extracurricular activities, are designed to help broaden children's skills and abilities and to give them a chance to practice leadership and assume responsibility, to supplement school courses, and to provide additional stimuli. These activities are another way for you to remain involved in your child's school experiences — adult volunteers are usually in short supply.

There is often a range of activities from which to choose, particularly at the junior high and high school levels. Nature clubs, musical organizations, science clubs, art and drama groups, or language clubs are common, as is a wide selection of sports activities. Virtually every high school has a student-run newspaper, often with a photographic darkroom. Some extracurricular activities take place during the school day, but many are held after classes are over. Even though they are optional, they are considered a part of the American educational experience. Parents encourage their children to participate in those programs that best suit their own special talents and interests. Students learn a great deal during these activities, especially in terms of relationships, social and intellectual skills, and a well-trained body.

Both employers and college admissions officers in the United States carefully consider the extracurricular activities in which students have participated, both during their free time after school and also during the long holidays. These are indicators of a young person's leadership potential, enthusiasm, creativity, breadth of interest, vitality, and personality. These qualities are weighed, together with the student's or candidate's academic record, to assess intelligence, perseverance, and ability to use what he or she has learned.

Higher Education

The American system of higher education can be bewildering in its diversity. There are over 4,000 colleges and universities in the United States, about half of which are private rather than public, tax-supported institutions. There are essentially four broad categories of postsecondary educational institutions: (1) vocational or trade schools, (2) junior colleges (including most community colleges), (3) colleges, and (4) universities.

Trade Schools and Technical Colleges

Trade schools can be public or private and offer courses that are generally not considered to be at the college level. They are similar to the vocational high schools except that they are geared toward adults and may or may not require a high school diploma (or equivalent) for admission.

Junior Colleges and Community Colleges

Junior colleges were once a common element of U.S. higher education, but the rise of community colleges in the last half of the twentieth century has left few of them in place. They were designed to help students bridge the gap between high school and college and to offer coursework that is generally considered to be the equivalent of the first two years at a college or university. Community colleges also offer two years of course work, after which students receive either a two-year (associate) degree or transfer to a four-year college or university. Some junior and community colleges resemble vocational schools, others are very academic in their focus. Careful research is needed to determine the right fit.

Colleges

Colleges are four-year institutions leading to the bachelor of arts (or science) degree and have few if any graduate programs. There are both state and countless private colleges. Some of the most prestigious undergraduate institutions are colleges rather than world-famous universities. For example, Amherst, Williams, Swarthmore, and Wellesley are generally considered to be of the same caliber as Harvard, Princeton, and Stanford. There are a few colleges that still enroll only women (and even fewer — just two — that enroll only men).

Universities

Universities offer a range of graduate, professional, and research programs in addition to undergraduate degrees. Some of them enroll as many as 50,000 students. Tuition at most private institutions is considerably higher than at state-supported schools, but all have tuition charges that will appear high to people from most other countries. Remember that unless you are a permanent resident or U.S. citizen (or one of a few other immigration categories), most public financial aid is unavailable to you. Some states will offer the in-state tuition discount to all of its residents regardless of citizenship; others will not. Keep in mind, though, that there is considerable merit-based financial aid available from the institutions themselves.

In many countries it is very difficult to get into a university because of competitive entrance examinations but easy to graduate once you are admitted. In the United States, it is relatively easy to gain admission to many colleges or universities but often quite difficult to finish all course work successfully in order to graduate. Universities and colleges rated at the top academically are very competitive, but most high school graduates are able to find a college or university that matches their qualifications.

Summer Camps and Jobs

Partly because of summer heat but mostly because we began as an agricultural nation, summer holidays are very long. Children and youth get restless if they have nothing to do, especially when they are living in cramped city apartments. As a result, there are thousands of different kinds of summer camps for children. They are run by many organizations such as the Boy Scouts, Girl Scouts, YMCA, YWCA, or religious institutions. There are also many private camps, which, although expensive, provide horseback riding, skilled instruction in various specialties, wilderness trips, and the like.

Older teenagers are more likely to seek summer jobs or go off with their own age groups on camping or other trips. Many go backpacking in the mountains. Anyone living in a city apartment may want to encourage such summer prospects for their young people.

Many teenagers earn a portion of their college expenses by working during the summer at such jobs as deckhand, waiter, clerk, harvester, construction worker, camp counselor, baby-sitter, gas station attendant, telephone operator, or messenger. American teenagers are not concerned with status. Being unskilled, they try to find jobs at whatever level they can, seeking not only money but also experience. They learn work skills, responsibility, and the ability to take orders and to get along with a boss and new kinds of people. As they grow older and more competent, most teenagers get better jobs, probably still unskilled but more closely tied to their fields of interest — in hospitals, political headquarters, newspapers, schools, or wherever. Students from abroad should check carefully into visa regulations, however, if they want to use the long holidays in this way. The dean or foreign student adviser at any school should be able to offer advice here, but the visa question should be raised in one's home country before leaving.

20
Raising Teenagers

The affluence, independence, and social freedom of American youth are frightening to many visiting parents as they contemplate bringing young people into America's teenage world.

One of the most difficult things to accept is the fact that, to a large degree, youth in the United States set their own rules, regulations, and patterns — parents here have less to say than in most countries about their children's actions outside the home, especially after the magic age of sixteen (the age of a driver's license and often a car!). This independence is threatening to many parents from abroad, who sometimes react by forbidding their children to take part in American teenage activities, insisting instead that they come directly home from school and not go on evening "dates" or group outings.

It is difficult for a young person to be so excluded because in the United States there are no alternatives. Most teenagers date in one way or another. This is the way the transition is made here from parent-dominated family life to marriage, and it covers a long period of time.

From eight or nine years of age to about twelve, children's friendships are usually confined to members of the same sex, and they love to visit overnight in each other's houses. Children, especially girls but also boys, have "slumber parties" or "sleepovers." This merely means that they like to spend the night together in one of their houses under parental supervision. There is much giggling, whispering, possibly some cookie making, pillow fighting, and so on. It is noisy but harmless and is part of the growing-up process. In the summer, some boys or girls may want to sleep outdoors in a tent or tree house or on a "campout." To children of these ages, sleeping away from home marks the first stage of independence, and they like to be in groups.

The next stage is an interest in the opposite sex. Long before they are ready emotionally or financially to marry, teenagers start "hanging out" together, and then dating. Groups of young people gather in shopping malls or eating places or at each other's houses. They listen to music, watch videos, drink beer and soft drinks, and may or may not move on to stronger alcoholic drinks and drugs. After a period of decline, illegal drug use is on the rise among teens, and most experts urge open and frank discussions between parents and children on this topic. Even in the most affluent neighborhoods and best schools, illegal drugs are readily available. Parents should not think they can avoid these issues by putting their children in private schools or moving to the suburbs. Young people in this country need strong, supportive and open communication with their parents to help them make the right choices.

Premarital chastity is not considered the major virtue it once was, and by the time they graduate from high school, many teenagers are not virgins. Even though birth control devices are readily available, large numbers of teenagers engage in unprotected sex — and the incidence of teenage pregnancy and the transmission of sexually transmitted diseases is alarmingly high. Large numbers of young women seek abortions (itself a highly volatile issue among politicians and citizen groups), but a growing percentage of pregnant teenagers are choosing to keep their babies and raise them alone or with help from their families. Some high schools now offer day-care services for these babies so that their mothers can finish high school. Teenage pregnancy is a grave concern for parents and for American society overall. Not all young people are sexually active, and sex education and the fear of AIDS have made some difference in some teens' sexual behavior. There has actually been a decline in the rate of young people engaging in sexual intercourse. Unfortunately, however, this has been accompanied by an alarming increase in other sexual behaviors (such as oral sex, usually unprotected) by ever younger people. Perhaps most alarming are the following statistics from the Media Project:

- Nearly three million youth are infected with a sexually transmitted disease (STD) annually.

- AIDS is the sixth leading cause of death for young people age 15–24.

- Each year nearly half of all new HIV infections occur in people under age 25.

- By age 20, 80 percent of males and over 75 percent of females have had sexual intercourse.

- America's teen birth rate is eight times higher than rates in comparable European nations.[1]

One current political debate in the U.S. centers on what type of sex education young people should get. Proponents of so-called "abstinence-only" education believe that sex education should consist of nothing more than admonishments to refrain from sex, while others believe that a comprehensive program is in order, including birth control options and ways to prevent the transmission of sexually transmitted diseases.

It is interesting to note that youth generally set, and also obey, their own rules. These rules vary by locality and age group, but teenagers do set their own standards to a large degree. Some groups are quite strict within their own codes, others more relaxed. Fashions and fads (whatever is currently popular) vary by locality and to some extent also by economic level and social background. Fads come and go within a group, but everyone tends to shift at the same time, and anyone who does not is considered strange. The penalty for not conforming to the rules is likely to be loss of reputation, loss of popularity, or both.

Bullying has become a growing concern in our schools. The American Academy of Child and Adolescent Psychiatry states that 10 percent of schoolchildren are bullied on a regular basis at some time in their education. And it is not only boys who engage in this aggressive behavior. In *Odd Girl Out: The Hidden Culture of Aggression in Girls*, author Rachel Simmons chronicles the more subtle ways in which schoolgirls bully their peers.[2] Of course, this is not meant to alarm you. After all, 90 percent of all students are not bullied. You should be aware of the issues and the resources, however, should your child show signs of depression or reluctance to attend school, as bullying may indeed be the issue. Remember that there are plenty of nice kids, too. At any large school students are likely to be able to choose from among various kinds of groups, ranging all the way from what the young call "preppy" (that is, conformist conservative) to "jocks" (sports-minded), "nerd/geek" (academic), "artsy," "punk" (facial piercings and/or brightly colored hair), or "goth" (prone to wearing all-black clothing and wearing heavy make-up, both boys and girls). These groups are often identified by their unusual dress and hair or other styles. Although strong conformity is usual within each group, a young person is free to choose which kind of group he or she prefers to join. Interestingly, although young people in the U.S. will resist being labeled as a member of any one group, they are generally quick to label others.

Although Americans are known for their individualism, they are also "joiners." They enjoy organizing and belonging to groups to pursue their personal interests. This group orientation is especially strong among teenagers, and parents often become worried if their child likes to be alone more than others, or if their child doesn't have many friends. However, the young person who prefers to read or play the violin or be alone is quite free to do so and may, in fact, be given considerable silent respect by others for his or her independence.

The greatest parental worry is sure to be what group of friends their children become involved with, for peer pressure among some groups leads to alcohol or drug use. Drugs, especially the prevalent and inexpensive "crack" (an easily ingested form of cocaine), are disturbingly popular in the United States — at all ages, starting as young as eleven or twelve. Unfortunately, drugs are easy to obtain in or near virtually all schools, and students are under great pressure from their peers to try them. Many do, however, resist. In fact, there is at present a relatively strong counter-reaction among both young people and adults to drug and alcohol use, and in reality, the number of people who become addicted to drugs is small relative to the size of the population.

Parents are advised to talk quite freely with school counselors and other parents about the situation in a given school — before enrollment if possible. Teachers and administrators are all deeply concerned too. Some will talk with you honestly about these issues if you ask them, but others are either unaware of the extent of the problem or afraid to talk about it.

Many middle-class American youth are quite affluent. Some earn their spending money themselves. Teenagers often have cars, which is disturbing to some foreign visitors to whom an automobile is a luxury. In the United States, however, having a car is not necessarily considered luxurious living. Distances in this country are great, and public transportation is sometimes limited, especially outside major cities. Teenagers often need cars to get to jobs, attend classes, or meet their friends.

The majority of American young people are responsible, hardworking, and stable, despite the drug and alcohol problem and despite the fact that the contrary is regularly reported abroad. Unfortunately, those who are spoiled, irresponsible, apathetic, or disillusioned are sometimes more visible.

Many of the problems of youth result from the massive social changes that are being experienced in this country — not only drugs, but also high divorce rates, unemployment, insecurity, major shifts in population, and the breakdown of moral and sex codes.

The more one's children spend time with stable families, with people who are active in religious organizations or school or community affairs, or with people who have jobs, the less likely they will be to find themselves among disillusioned or irresponsible groups of young people. The more active they are in sports and other school activities, the more likely they are to be with other healthy-minded youth. The point is, though, that today parents cannot assume that all is well. They must be alert to what is going on in the school, in the neighborhood, and among their children's companions.

Despite worries over teenage morality in this open society, parents will find much that is good in the system, too. The depth and freedom of discussion, the vitality and initiative, a deep sense of public and community service among many, and the easy camaraderie of American youth can provide great experiences for your teenagers. They will inevitably take part in life with their school friends, and you should not try to prevent it. If they are made to seem "different" by parental decree, they may become rebellious or very lonely, for they will be cut off from their schoolmates.

You can exert an indirect influence, however. First, of course, you have the all-important choice of neighborhood and school. In addition you can encourage, in an inconspicuous way, certain of your children's friendships more than others. You can provide outside activities with different young people — ski trips, for example, or volunteer projects, or a photography class, or summer excursions. You should get to know your child's school and other parents, join the parent-teacher group, attend all school functions, and offer your services on school committees. The more you take part in the school life, the more you will understand your child and his or her friends.

You should not come to America worried about your children. As stated above, the majority of American young people are serious-minded and responsible. Undeniably, however, in this troubled world, youth is restless everywhere, and problems do arise. Since American parents as well as visitors are naturally concerned about any difficulties their children may be experiencing, there are many sources of advice and guidance, all of which are freely available to any parent. If you are concerned, you will be able to ask advice.

Most public libraries have "young adult" sections. Librarians will help you find useful information if you ask for their help. As in every other phase of adjusting to this new culture, you should feel free to ask those around you for their ideas and advice. You will find other parents interested in your thoughts, your problems, and your reactions to youth issues in the United States. They will not be embarrassed to discuss the subject, and you need feel no hesitation either. Remember, though, that parents' roles in this country might be different from those in your country. Just as your children are learning to live in a new culture, you must also do the same. This doesn't mean a breakdown of the values you adhere to, but it does mean trying to understand other values that you see represented all around you.

One loss that many new families experience in the United States is the loss of an extended family network. In many countries grandparents, aunts and uncles, and older cousins all play important roles in each others' children's lives. Without an older cousin or longtime friend to talk with, your children might feel that they can't turn to anyone to discuss their problems. This is not a reflection on you or your parenting — there are things that most young people have trouble talking about with their parents. One option readily available here is a therapist or counselor. These trained professionals can help teenagers sort through their thoughts and feelings about growing up, moving away from home, and navigating a new world of choices. Therapists in this country are not reserved for serious mental problems — anyone can visit a counselor for a few visits or longer without any stigma associated with it. Nearly all schools, for example, have counselors. It is the job of these men and women to advise either students or parents who are perplexed or experiencing difficulties in any way. It might be wise for you and your children to go together to talk with your school's counselor soon after your arrival, well before there are any problems. Ask the counselor about the local dating situation, the prevalence of drug and alcohol use, school activities, and areas of concern in both the community and the school. Then you can plan your choices instead of just finding your way by chance.

Another difficulty many parents are experiencing is setting appropriate limits on computer use. Young people use computers for instant messaging with their friends or hanging out in Internet chat rooms, spending valuable time you might think is being spent on studying. Also worrisome is the ease with which even very young children can gain access to the most vivid pornographic images. There are numerous computer tools to help you place reasonable controls on your children's computer use. Programs such as NetNanny and Surfwatch can be particularly useful.

21

Finding Friends and Having Fun

Because Americans play hard and rather loudly, a visitor's first impression may be one of mass fun and games — of campers rolling down the highways, crowded beaches, packed baseball stadiums, endless television. In order to understand the true picture of how Americans use their leisure, however, you need to look below this noisy surface.

The Land of Leisure Time?

Since machines have accelerated work in homes as well as in factories, one might think that both men and women have more free time than ever before in our history. In reality, Americans work an average of 55 hours per week, more than in any other industrialized country according to economist Juliet Schor in her book *The Overworked American*.[1] It is true, of course, that much leisure time is used for playing. It is a country of sports — hunting, fishing, swimming, sailing, tennis, and golf are available at all prices to all people. Americans by the millions love both to play and to watch team sports like baseball and football. They bowl, run or jog, ride bicycles, ski, or follow active sports of every kind. Also, they watch television by the millions, take part in community orchestras, make their own films or recordings, go camping, travel, garden, cook, read books, pursue many crafts and hobbies, and play video games. Being part of a do-it-yourself country, people enjoy building their own shelves or boats, sewing their own clothes, or developing their own film; they do such things for fun as well as for economy.

America is a "self-improvement" country. More than twenty-five million adults are enrolled in one kind of course or another, mostly on their own time, at their own expense. If you doubt the do-it-yourself mindset of U.S. Americans, visit a Home Depot or HQ superstore and watch people purchasing everything from nails to electrical wire to house paint.

Volunteering

In addition to the time spent on personal pursuits, Americans volunteer a tremendous amount of time for the varied needs of their communities. It has been said that if all the volunteers of the country withdrew, the nation would come to a halt. This would include people working in hospitals, schools, libraries, museums, playgrounds, community centers, welfare projects, clinics, and so on. Why do so many Americans volunteer to work long, hard hours, often at dull and disagreeable work, without pay? What is their motive?

There are several answers. The concept of cooperating for mutual benefit, a sense of interlocking responsibility, and a willingness to work together are all deeply rooted in American history. The original pioneer settlers had to work together to survive. They had crossed dangerous seas and risked all they had in their struggle for political and religious freedom. They helped each other clear land, build homes, and harvest crops. Americans have traditionally valued their freedom and independence, and they still do. Deep-seated distrust of central government still remains in all aspects of American life. People still prefer to do things themselves within their communities rather than give a government agency control or wait for its bureaucratic delays.

Sometimes Americans volunteer because they want to achieve something for which no money is paid. So they come together to contribute their energies — as is also done elsewhere. They may work together to put a new roof on a church, to send parcels to flood victims, to provide summer holidays for underprivileged children, to build a new playground, or to clean up a polluted stream. People will give time after a long, hard day to work on a town zoning commission, school board, or planning committee. They care about their towns.

Hundreds of thousands of so-called leisure hours go into hard, sustained, unpaid work on one or another community need. As you read the local newspapers, you will see that Americans are constantly forming new kinds of citizens' groups for some of the following reasons: to improve the lot of migrant workers, to take action against some form of discrimination, to fight crime, to elect an official, to protect consumers from fraud, to fight against drugs or drunk driving, or to do away with a pesticide that is killing wildlife.

One does not need to be a citizen to join in such activities. Once you settle into a community (even a big city), you will soon be aware of the varieties of volunteer projects going on around you. Anyone who is interested in sharing this side of American life will greatly deepen his or her understanding of the country. You can start by calling a volunteer center or contacting a local church, temple, mosque, synagogue, community center, or other organization. Asking neighbors about what is available often elicits a helpful response. Or if you read about something that interests you in the local paper, contact the organization and offer your time or help. Most people welcome assistance if they do not have to pay for it. This kind of volunteering may open interesting doors to you as well. As mentioned in Chapter 19, many schools and colleges include volunteer opportunities in their curricula. See Chapter 5 for more information about how we Americans volunteer our time.

Organizations and Interest Groups

Perhaps in your home country you already belong to some group such as Rotary International, Lions, an association of university women, or a professional group (of journalists, chemical engineers, doctors, and so on). Perhaps you belong to a sports club — ski, tennis, soccer, or hiking. Many overseas universities have alumni chapters scattered around the United States.

If you are already a member of an organization at home, look for its affiliate here and let them know of your desire to participate. You will get an immediate welcome. If you are interested in (but not yet affiliated with) a group, try to become a member before leaving your own country. You will then automatically be eligible to join activities with your American counterparts on arrival without waiting for membership formalities. Such channels for making new friends will be most useful when you first arrive, so it is good to come with introductions and with memberships already established, if you can.

There are, of course, many sports and activities that anyone can engage in without joining formal organizations. Hunting and fishing enthusiasts can find colleagues here in great numbers, as can climbers, hikers, skiers, bridge players, photographers, chess players, ham radio enthusiasts, birdwatchers, or cellists! Whatever your nationality, you can also find a national group in any large city. Ask at your nearest consulate or look under "Associations" in the Yellow Pages to find the Turkish Society, India House, African Center, or whatever exists locally.

Classes and Lectures

Perhaps for a while when you first come to the States, you will want to study English or join an English conversation group in order to gain confidence in speaking. Or perhaps you will have time to acquire some new skills or to take a short course that has always interested you.

Adult education is widespread. Classes are offered in a wide range of subjects: painting, cooking, photography, languages, astronomy, computer programming. One need not necessarily have any particular qualifications to enroll in these classes. Or you may be interested in taking more substantive courses leading to degrees, certificates, or diplomas. Just a few possibilities of subject areas are journalism, interior decorating, fashion design, business administration, accounting, and so on.

Both formal and informal classes are advertised in local newspapers. Look under "Schools" in the Yellow Pages. Jewish Community Centers, YMCAs, YWCAs, and community or neighborhood centers, offer a wide range of classes; the public school systems of most cities sponsor adult evening classes, as do community colleges. Ask for a catalogue of adult courses from the local board of education.

In addition, if you are near any of the nation's 4,000 colleges and universities, you will find they make courses, concerts, and lectures available to the nearby community. Usually these are held in the evening. You can ask to be put on their mailing list for advance notice.

Many Americans attend lectures. If you like to be intellectually stimulated but do not have time for a complete course, you can follow any line of interest on a more casual basis — often free. You may want to explore new fields like oceanography, city planning, or outer space.

In addition to lectures given at colleges and universities, you will find that botanical gardens, civil rights organizations, government and political groups, churches, and museums also offer a great number of lectures, debates, and forums; so do international organizations, business groups, and professional organizations.

Get yourself on mailing lists (usually free for the asking), listen to local radio announcements, or ask your friends' advice. Easiest of all — just read the newspapers.

Museums

If your idea of a museum is a dusty row of glass cases or rooms full of badly lit oil paintings, try going to some of the museums in U.S. cities and towns. The art of display itself has become highly developed in this country, so that museums have come alive to an extraordinary degree in recent years.

In addition to many fine art museums, look also for natural history or science museums. Children's museums are sprouting up all over the country and usually offer a wide range of fascinating, "hands-on" exhibits. Photographic exhibits are often a particularly good way to understand the social concerns of a country. Don't miss the many small museums of contemporary crafts, African American history, Native American history, musical instruments, or coins. While at the museum you can often join a group tour or rent a small tape-recorded guide, which will add much to your understanding (rental fees are generally modest). Sometimes they are available in several languages. Those going to Boston, New York, Philadelphia, Washington, D.C., Atlanta, Chicago, Denver, Los Angeles, or San Francisco should plan to spend considerable time at the particularly fine museums in these cities.

Places like Williamsburg, Virginia, Dearborn, Michigan, and Sturbridge Village, Massachusetts, are whole villages, reconstructed as living museums to depict the life of our early settlers. At most times of the year there are live demonstrations of many old crafts, such as candle making, quilting, or the shoeing of horses. There are waterfront museums at Mystic, Connecticut, and the seaports of New York and Baltimore, where one may have the opportunity to board old sailing vessels. The old Spanish missions in California trace the history of Spanish settlements in south-western United States. Smaller cities almost always have some sort of museum depicting the history of the area; Palm Springs, California, and Phoenix and Tucson, Arizona, for example, have desert museums.

The Performing Arts

The United States abounds in theater, music, and dance, both professional and amateur. Most large cities have their own symphony orchestras; there is a wealth of experimental music and drama being produced across the country in college theaters, community centers, and small neighborhood theaters. Traditional theater and music are also plentiful. Even if you do not live in New York City, you can see the Broadway favorites. Touring companies produce excellent, professional-quality performances in most large- and medium-sized cities throughout the country. For the fine arts, try to buy season tickets if you will be in the same town for a while. Not only will you save money, you will be sure to have a seat at even the most popular productions.

Tickets are often sold at the box office but also online and usually through agencies such as Ticketron and Ticketmaster. Beware of "scalpers" who sell tickets to sold-out events at inflated prices. Not only is the practice illegal, it often involves fake tickets. Imagine your disappointment when you come to an event, only to find that your tickets are no good! There are some legitimate ticket brokers, who advertise their services in the arts and leisure section of the newspaper. They get around scalping laws by operating in a state other than the one where the event is held. Prices are still inflated, but at least the tickets are genuine.

Movies, of course, are very popular in the United States, and there are many film festivals in medium and large cities. Many universities show foreign films, and this can be one of the few venues available for seeing them in a smaller town.

Sports

Newcomers to the United States often find it difficult to participate in the particular sports they enjoy. Actually, it need not be so. Almost all sports are available everywhere, even in a crowded city such as New York. One of the first places to investigate if you are interested in swimming, tennis, badminton, gym classes, modern dance, or any indoor sports is the nearest Jewish Community Center, YMCA, or YWCA. Most of these are well equipped and provide excellent facilities for reasonable fees. There are fancier and more expensive facilities for all such sports as well, often at clubs or hotels. Also, don't forget that any good bookstore has books on virtually every kind of sporting or recreational (including travel) activity by locality. Some colleges and universities also sell memberships to their indoor sports facilities, which are often of excellent quality.

Swimming

Many swimming pools are open to the public. In addition to those run by the YWCA or YMCA, others are operated by the cities or towns themselves or by hotels or swimming schools. When weather permits, there are often public pools and beaches available within a reasonable distance. Usually these can be reached by public transport — either bus or train — as well as by private car. Look in the Yellow Pages under "Swimming" or "Sports."

Other Sports

Read the newspapers or look in the telephone book under the name of whatever sport interests you: ski clubs; walking clubs; fencing, gymnastics, judo, karate, and aerobics classes; ice skating; squash and racquetball clubs; bicycle clubs; bowling clubs; riding groups; and bird-watching clubs. Golf and tennis are very popular. In addition to private clubs, nearly all cities maintain numerous tennis courts and golf courses, which are open to the public for a fee. Soccer (football) has gained popularity in recent years, especially in programs for children. Cricket, however, is still very hard to find, although not impossible. Ask your local Department of Parks and Recreation for booklets describing its sports facilities or visit the Chamber of Commerce or the Visitors Center.

Those who like baseball need only drift around the parks. Many games will be going on. Employees often form softball or baseball teams connected with different departments and have a full schedule of games. Usually they need, and welcome, additional players. Roller-skating, Frisbee throwing, and kite flying are all popular, especially in parks; one can also find paths for biking, jogging, or walking in these areas. However, it is not wise to visit many parks after dark.

Spectator Sports

Many Americans prefer to watch sports rather than to participate in them. American football, basketball, and hockey all have devoted fans, but baseball is considered the national sport. Soccer has also gained a growing audience in this country.

In addition to the endless seasons of professional sporting events, there are often second-tier events such as minor league baseball, where smaller cities pit their teams against one another. College and even high school sports are enormously popular spectator opportunities as well.

Camping and Hiking

In most locations you will find excellent camping facilities in both state and national parks as well as in nearby private campgrounds.

You can get free booklets and maps describing public camping facilities and park areas by writing to both the individual state parks department and the National Park Service in Washington, D.C. When you write, state your specific interests. Information centers along major highways or in towns also offer booklets or maps of both public and private camping and recreational vehicle facilities. Each state also has a Visitors' Bureau, which you can call or write to request information on recreational opportunities there.

All over the United States, there are thousands of miles of walking trails, all kinds of lodges and huts for hikers, and a great many campsites where you can pitch tents and find water, but you need to know where to find them in order to avoid overcrowded highways and too many people. You need to make reservations months ahead in the most popular public parks such as the Grand Canyon and Yellowstone. However, millions of acres of national forest land are available for hiking and camping without prior permission. A parking permit is usually all that is required. Compared with hiking trails in Europe, most of ours remain blissfully uncrowded. For the national parks, check out the highly informational Website at www.nps.gov/, and for the national forests, see www.fs.fed.us/.

Fishing and Hunting

The state and national booklets mentioned above also include information on fishing and hunting. Both activities are highly regulated with regard to location, season, equipment, species, and the number of catches or kills you can make. Check local regulations to avoid problems. Many fishing areas are "catch and release" only. You can always find fellow enthusiasts in your own locality. Talk to your colleagues, read the sports columns in the newspapers, or chat with salespeople in the sporting goods stores. Through such contacts you can find out what clubs there are in the vicinity and then ask about the possibility of joining one. Public-owned facilities are sometimes crowded; joining a group or club gives you access to more private waters and woods. Most clubs have reasonably open membership rules and would welcome your inquiry. They range in price from moderate to high; the lower the price, the more welcoming they are in general, but also the more crowded. The expensive clubs are, of course, likely to be the most exclusive.

If you are a deep-sea fishing enthusiast, there are boats and captains ready to take you out at almost any marina or port. Prices per day are high, but if you form a group and go together, you can divide the cost among many of you.

Bird Watching

Those interested in birds should look up the nearest Audubon Society in the telephone book and ask about groups, activities, or sanctuaries in the area. The local library is another good source of information.

Watching Americans at Work

There are many people who do not want to become deeply involved in American activities but who are still interested in learning about the country. If you are among this group, you are welcome to take tours of workplaces. It is easy to watch a nation work when you visit people at their jobs.

If you cannot find out about possibilities through your friends, just call the place of business that most interests you (factory, farm, store, etc.) and ask for the public relations department. They will be able to tell you whether they have tours (some factories schedule them regularly) or whether you can visit on your own. Tell them where you are from and why you are interested. In most cases you will find that people are friendly and pleased to have you visit as their guest, although they may first check with your office to make sure you are who you say you are. Your local Chamber of Commerce and city information center are also good sources.

Since 2001, many places that used to be open for public tours — power plants, water treatment facilities, and the like — are very reluctant to permit public access. In addition, we have in general become more cautious about unexpected visits by strangers, so be sure to make arrangements in advance. This way people know you are coming, and you can know that your visit will be convenient for them. Then, *be on time.* If you must be late, be sure to telephone. You generally do not tip or pay any fee (except for factories that have become tourist attractions), but a thank-you letter afterward will be much appreciated.

You can visit most kinds of factories and watch men and women working at heavy industry, precision manufacturing, or food processing. You can call on various kinds of schools, watch courts in progress, listen to hearings before government committees, and attend town meetings or meetings of school boards. Rarely are any of these private. Usually the public is admitted, although sometimes only by previous arrangement. Often there are tours for the public "behind the scenes" in such places as department stores, post offices, or newspaper plants. Again, contact the local Chamber of Commerce.

In this country you should not be shy or retiring. A little effort on your part will provide you with a great deal of insight into the American way of life. We welcome guests, we are flattered to have people interested in what we are doing, and we are proud to show them what we have.

22

Twenty-First-Century Issues

The United States of the early twenty-first century faces serious issues. The end of the Cold War has left us with the obligation to seek out a new paradigm. If you make this country your home, even for just a few years, they will become your issues are well.

The Effect of September 11, 2001

For many Americans, perhaps for most of us, the tragic events of September 11, 2001, "changed everything." On that day, foreigners attacked and killed thousands of civilians in our country. Certain aspects of that day are likely to continue to influence our political and social outlook for many years to come. We naively believed that such a large-scale attack was not possible here. We also believed that some people hate us solely because we are Americans. The hijackers all legally entered our country and lived among us, some of them for years.

The fact that we in the United States have lost our innocence is resonating throughout our geopolitical world. Fear is driving our politics, and to some degree, the rest of our lives as well. Most Americans have a great deal of difficulty understanding how one person can hate another because of his or her nationality. After all, we see ourselves as individuals first, and only then as Americans. And as Americans, we believe that while not perfect, we are always well-intentioned. Perhaps most of all, many Americans were shocked that the hijackers entered the country perfectly legally. What many of us found the hardest to believe is that anyone could live among us — some of them for years — and still hate us so much. After all, aren't we a friendly people? Isn't this the land of opportunity? We wonder, "Couldn't they see that for all our corporate scandals and foreign policy mistakes, we really mean well?"

Fear and doubt, then, are driving our national agenda. There is a political voice in this country that asks whether 9/11 is at least partly a result of a country that has gone soft, weak, and too willing to let anyone into this country. Attempts to restrict immigration and to punish those who immigrate illegally are underway. There are, sadly, many Americans who feel that our government is justified in considering all Arabs and Muslims a threat. Juxtaposed to this, Islam is the fastest-growing religion in the United States, spurred partly by the tremendous curiosity many Americans feel about the religion, a curiosity that turns into respect and admiration for a faith practiced by a quarter of the world's population.

Threats to our civil liberties are being accepted on a daily basis, despite the warning, often attributed to Benjamin Franklin, "Those who would sacrifice their essential liberties for a little safety will soon have neither." Government officials continue to appear with disturbing regularity to announce some new vague threat to our lives. Our color-coded Terror Alert System blinks from yellow to orange and back again, despite the fact that almost no one knows what it means.

Not all of the effects of 9/11 are based on fear and doubt, however. A significant segment of society has begun a process of self-reflection to a degree not seen before. Many people are asking themselves questions such as, what policies are we, as a nation, engaged in that could breed such hatred? What liberties are we willing to forgo in order to feel safer and more secure, and which ones are we not willing to give up? And our strong sense of individualism means that most of us are willing, even eager, to assess each individual we meet on his or her own characteristics.

The Impact of the War in Iraq

World sympathy for the United States was genuine and heartfelt in the weeks following 9/11. When the U.S. military dismantled the Taliban in Afghanistan and destroyed the camps used to train terrorists, the world largely supported us. But the U.S. decision to launch a pre-emptive, all-out war in Iraq, despite the reservations of much of the world, has inflamed passions against the United States. Even some of our staunchest allies no longer support us.

This is not to say that George W. Bush made the wrong decision when he opted to invade Iraq without the world's support. The point is that regardless of what any of us thinks about the decision to go to war when we did (and the way we did it), we must accept the fact that much of the world disapproves of our action. This shift in the way the rest of the world views us will have a profound effect on our relationships for many years to come. Within eighteen months of the French newspaper *Le Monde*'s headline, "We are all Americans," an overwhelming portion of the world no longer views us with sympathy, but with fear and distrust.

The torture and other abuses of Iraqi prisoners have further eroded the world's opinions of the United States — and, I daresay, our opinions about ourselves. The claim of moral authority, long suspect to much of the world, is at last being widely questioned at home as well.

The Rise of Religious Fundamentalism

As discussed in Chapter 6, the United States is a land of religious pluralism. Protestants, Catholic, and other Christian groups have by and large laid the foundation for a society that includes Mormons, Muslims, Buddhists, Jains, Sikhs, Hindus, Wiccans, and countless other faiths.

Religious fundamentalists (those who believe that their version of their faith has a monopoly on virtue) are increasing both in their numbers and in their influence. Just as Islamic fundamentalists, a tiny fringe of the world's billion-plus Muslims, are increasing in their numbers and influence around the world, Christian fundamentalists are threatening to end the equality of faiths in this country. People of faith, quite understandably, view their religion as the best possible path. But when they begin to view it as the *only* possible path, taking it to the extreme of using their political, military, or physical power to punish those who believe differently, it threatens everyone.

Segregation, Polarization, and "Pernicious" Dualism

Americans are more segregated than ever. We are segregated by race and ethnicity, by class, and increasingly, by politics. We are diverse as a country, but we live in neighborhoods with people who are more and more like us. As journalist David Brooks observed, "Block by block, and institution by institution, we are remarkably homogenous."[1]

Because we are such a geographically mobile country, we have frequent opportunities to make choices about where we will live. Progressives and liberals are drawn to Boston and San Francisco, while conservatives might be more likely to choose Texas. The realignments seem to be moving us into more and more politically homogeneous states as well.

Dualism is the idea that there are only two ways to look at any problem, situation, or the world. American culture is, by its very nature, rather dualistic. We tend to see things as either black or white. Either we are friends or we are not. Either something is right or it is wrong. A person is either good or evil. This position does not allow us to accept shades of gray or a middle ground when approaching complex situations.

Pernicious dualism, a term often used by Columbia University Teachers' College professor L. Lee Knefelkamp, refers to the tendency of some people to exploit dualism to their advantage (the word *pernicious* means "done with evil intent.").[2] *Either you support the war or you are unpatriotic. You are either with us, or you are "with the terrorists." Those who oppose the U.S. occupation of Iraq "hate freedom."* And pernicious dualists are not always political conservatives; liberals can be just as limiting in their framing of problems. *Either you support Affirmative Action or you are a racist. Either you support abortion rights or you are a woman hater.* The list on both sides goes on.

However, as linguist George Lakoff has observed, the political right is far more effective in naming issues and programs in order to force a dualistic response.[3] Who could be against a "healthy forest initiative" or against laws with names like the "patriot" act or the "defense of marriage" act? Obviously, only a person who is an anti-marriage, tree-hating traitor could oppose these, never mind that these issues were, respectively, about increasing logging on public land, curbing civil liberties, and denying millions of committed same-sex couples the right to marry. Again, the point here is not that these programs were themselves without any merits, only that in naming them the way they did, their proponents were able to cut short vital debate about their strengths and weaknesses.

If Americans cannot become more comfortable with nuance, complexity, and relativism, we become more likely to fall into the pernicious dualist's trap. We lose the ability to think clearly and creatively about complex problems and will tend to increasingly rely on those with the most extreme positions to define our issues and limit our solutions. This polarization in our thinking, further promoted by our two-party monopoly on national politics, is making us as a country more divided.

Globalization and Corporate Power

Americans, like many people around the world, have a "love-hate" relationship with globalization. Of course we, like many people, enjoy buying high-quality goods at lower prices. Of course we also object when employers close up manufacturing or, increasingly, high-tech facilities and then move those jobs to countries that hire workers at lower wages. We also do not like to see companies fatten their profits by avoiding environmental or safety regulations when they move to other countries. We like to talk about free trade but overlook our own protections on agricultural and other goods. We have faith in the free market but tend to forget that historically, all major economies, including our own, advanced as a result of stiff tariffs and other means of protecting domestic industries.

The power that corporations are able to exert over the political process is staggering. While some hail the collapse of Enron and the financial scandals of other corporations as evidence that the bad guys do get caught, it is more likely that they represent the tip of the iceberg. Corporate influence on the electoral process, and the resulting access to politicians (of both parties), threatens to undermine our treasured democratic ideals.

Health Care and Retirement

As discussed in Chapter 11, health-care costs have spiraled out of control. Millions of Americans do not have any health insurance, and those who do are largely not willing to give up what they have in exchange for a more equitable system. For the most part, we believe that we have the best health care in the world, and we want to hang onto it at any cost.

Furthermore, as mentioned in Chapter 3, the U.S. population is aging. Our medical care system will be crushed along with the national pension system, called Social Security, unless significant structural reform is achieved. By most estimates, the Social Security system will stop generating a surplus around 2020 and will exhaust its trust fund by the year 2034. Many Americans do not rely on Social Security, depending instead on privately funded pension plans. This means that the poor will by far bear the biggest share of this hardship.

World Leadership

The end of the cold war has brought more violence to the world than when there were two large, stabilizing forces looming at one another in the form of the Warsaw Pact and the North Atlantic Treaty Organization. Most Americans are uncomfortable with playing the role of the world's policeman, but threats to our own interests as well as a fear of a world without military leadership allow many of us to be persuaded to commit military forces to places like Bosnia and Iraq. Many Americans either distrust the United Nations outright, or else they generally support the UN, but fear that it is ineffective in a crisis. We are, at best, ambivalent about the role of the United States in relation to the rest of the world.

Energy, Water, and the Environment

The American appetite for energy, primarily in the form of oil, promises to pose serious political and economic stress for many years to come. The United States does not produce enough petroleum to satisfy our appetite, making us dependent on foreign sources. We have low gasoline prices and a love affair with large vehicles. Proponents of energy independence are sharply divided on how to proceed. One faction wishes to exploit more oil reserves in the U.S., primarily in Alaska, while others are unwilling to sacrifice national wildlife preserves for what is at best a temporary solution. Unwilling to seriously subsidize mass transit and pedestrian paths and bikeways, the United States spends some 200 million dollars *per day* on road construction.

The United States has about 4 percent of the world's population, and consumes a quarter of the world's energy. Of course, other highly industrial countries also disproportionately consume energy. For each dollar of gross domestic product, however, the U.S. consumes about 40 percent more energy than Japan or the European Union.

Global climate change has directed our attention to the coming crisis in water allocation. The Southwestern desert has virtually bloomed with agricultural expansion as a result of the dam projects of the last century. But while agricultural use is expected to be reduced, the municipal demand in places like Nevada and Arizona is expected to continue to increase. These hot, dry areas are the fast-growing population centers in the U.S.

Privacy

The ease with which your identity can be stolen is indeed alarming. Perhaps just as alarming is the ease with which many facts — long considered personal facts — can be made known to the public. For a small fee, there are companies that will scour the Internet for your name and address, the school attended by your children, the purchase price of your home, or any number of other pieces of information. These are things that have long been a matter of public record but which now can be compiled in a matter of minutes rather than the days of personal trips to various government offices and waiting in lines, or separate inquiries by letter punctuated by many months for responses.

Even more alarming is the amount of information that your employer can legally collect. Your e-mails, telephone calls, and office space are all legal places for your employer to observe your behavior.

The Patriot Act, a law that allows law enforcement officials to gather information more quickly and share it with other agencies, was intended to stop terrorists. However, these broad powers can be used on anyone without the due process of seeking a judge's permission. Government officials can listen in on private telephone conversations, access private e-mails, even listen to conversations in your home. Some of these new provisions are set to expire December 31, 2005, but the current administration is seeking to make them permanent.

The Wealth Gap

The last decades of the twentieth century might be summed up as "the rich got richer, the poor got poorer." Consider the following, from the United Nations Development Program. Microsoft's top three officers (Bill Gates, Paul Allen, and Steve Ballmer) have more assets than the combined gross national product of the 43 least-developed countries. In addition, the 200 richest people in the world more than doubled their net worth between 1994 and 1998, but in nearly half the world's countries, per capita incomes are lower now than they were ten or twenty years ago.[4] And this is not just a case of a rich country getting richer. The inequality in wealth is also evident within the United States. According to New York University economist Edward Wolff, the wealthiest 5 percent of Americans now own 59 percent of the country's net worth.[5] That may be less skewed than in many other countries, but the trend here runs counter to our cherished notion of a classless society. And, as Berkeley sociologist Manuel Castells has observed, the poverty rate has continued to rise in the United States, creating a "Dual America."[6]

Conclusion

We are, perhaps above all else, an optimistic people. The twenty-first century will continue to bring challenges to the United States and, indeed, the entire world. You will find in our population such a diverse set of opinions on a variety of matters that you will be hard pressed to determine just what is the American viewpoint. In the end, however, despite periods of challenges, we tend to look always toward the future, for a better country and a better world.

Appendix A

National Holidays

In general, whenever one of these holidays falls on Saturday or Sunday, the following Monday is celebrated as the official holiday. Exceptions to this are New Year's Day and Christmas Day. For a particular year, consult www.opm.gov/fedhol/.

New Year's Day, January 1st

Birthday of Martin Luther King, Civil Rights Leader, the third Monday in January

Inauguration Day, January 20th every four years

Presidents' Day, the third Monday in February

Memorial Day, the last Monday in May, to honor those who died while serving in the military

Flag Day, June 14th (businesses generally remain open)

Independence Day, July 4

Labor Day, the first Monday in September

Columbus Day, the second Monday in October

Election Day, Tuesday on or after November 2 (businesses generally remain open)

Veterans' Day, November 11th (businesses generally remain open)

Thanksgiving Day, the fourth Thursday in November (many businesses remain closed the following day as well, except for retail stores, which have enormous pre-Christmas sales)

Christmas Day, December 25th

Appendix B

Conversions

Americans' stubborn resistance, even hostility, toward the metric system is sure to frustrate most visitors and newcomers. Hopefully, these conversions will help.

Temperature

To change Fahrenheit into Celsius subtract 32 and multiply by $\frac{5}{9}$: $(F-32) \times \frac{5}{9} = C$.

Here are some examples.

Fahrenheit	Celsius
0°	−18°
32°	0°
50°	10°
68°	20° (room temp.)
86°	30°
104°	40°
212°	100° (boiling)
98.6°	37° (body temperature)

Weights and Measures

mile   a little over two kilometers; multiply kilometers by .6 to get miles

yard	just short of a meter, a meter is $^{11}/_{10}$ of a yard; one meter is 3.2 feet (a yard is 3 feet)
foot	30.4 centimeters; 3 feet equals one yard
inch	about 3 centimeters (a centimeter is $^{3}/_{10}$ of an inch); one U.S. foot is 12 inches
quart	almost the size of a liter (the liter is $^{11}/_{10}$ of a quart); gasoline is sold by the gallon, which is four quarts
pint	almost a half liter (2 pints equals 1 quart)
pound	approximately one-half kilogram; a kilogram is actually 2.2 pounds
ounce	approximately 30 grams; there are 16 ounces in a pound; for measures smaller than an ounce, Americans divide the ounce: ½ ounce, ¼ ounce, and so forth.

Clothing Sizes

Throughout the world there is an attempt to standardize sizes. However, there is still so much variation that shopping is always difficult when one first moves to another country.

Even with a size-conversion chart, you would do well to shop with your tape measure in hand and, above all, try clothing on. Body shapes, fullness, armholes, proportion of body size to neck band or sleeve length vary according to national origin. If your size is not "standard" by American measures, you may have to search a bit among unfamiliar terms such as "junior," "petite," "plus" (women), and "big and tall" (men). Large department stores often have what they call "Personal Shopping Departments" or "Service Desks" where you can get help if you ask for it. Many major stores in large cities have salespeople who can speak a number of languages.

The following comparison of American with European sizes may be helpful to Asians, Africans, or South Americans as well, since many countries follow either British or continental measurements. Please realize, however, that there is considerable variation from country to country and even within countries. The information below, therefore, is included only as a guide and is not to be taken necessarily as an exact measure.

Women

Suits, Dresses, and Coats

U.S.A.	8	10	12	14	16	18	20
British	10 (34)	12 (36)	14 (38)	16 (40)	18 (42)	20 (44)	22
Continental	38	40	42	44	46	48	

Sweaters, T-shirts, and Other Tops

Small	Sizes under 10
Medium	Sizes 10–12
Large	Sizes 14–16
Extra Large	Sizes 18–20

In skirts, dresses, and coats, half sizes are usually intended for the short-waisted, stocky figure.

Stockings

U.S.A.	8	8½	9	9½	10	10½
British	8	8½	9	9½	10	10½
Continental	0	1	2	3	4	5

(But many European countries use the same sizes as the United States.)

Shoes

U.S.A.	6	6½	7	7½	8	8½
British	4½	5	5½	6	6½	7
Continental	38	38	39	39	40	41

Men

Suits and Overcoats

U.S.A.	36	38	40	42	44	46
British	36	38	40	42	44	46
Continental	46	48	50	52	54	56

Shirts

U.S.A.	14½	15	15½	16	16½
European	37	38	39	40	41

Sweaters, T-shirts, and Some Shirts

Small	Sizes under 36 British or U.S.A. or 46 European
Medium	36–38 British or 46–48 European
Large	40 British or European
Extra Large	anything over 40 British or European

Shoes and Slippers

U.S.A.	8	8½	9½	10½	11½	12
British	7	7½	8½	9½	10½	11
European	41	42	43	44	45	46

Americans often use the sizes Small, Medium, Large, or Extra Large.

Translating Cooking Measures

Since recipes and measures will often be given in what will at first be unfamiliar terms, be *sure* to bring your own measuring spoons and cups. Americans rarely use scales in home cooking. The following may be helpful.

1 teaspoon = ⅓ tablespoon

3 teaspoons = 1 tablespoon

2 tablespoons = 1 fluid ounce

4 tablespoons = ¼ cup

8 tablespoons = ½ cup

16 tablespoons = 8 fluid ounces = ½ pint = 1 cup

2 cups = 16 fluid ounces = 1 pint = 1 pound

2 pints = 1 quart

4 quarts, liquid = 1 gallon, liquid

8 quarts = 1 peck (dry measure)

Metric Measure by Weight

1 ounce = 30 grams

16 ounces = 1 pound = 454 grams

2 pounds and 3 ounces = 1 kilogram or kilo

14 pounds = 1 stone = 6.36 kilograms

100 grams = 3.5 ounces

200 grams = 7 ounces

400 grams = 14 ounces

454 grams = 16 ounces = 1 pound

Metric Measure by Fluid Volume

1 dram = ¾ teaspoon = ⅛ ounce = 3.7 milliliters

1 teaspoon = ⅙ ounce = 5 milliliters

1 tablespoon = ½ ounce = 15 milliliters

8 tablespoons = ½ cup

16 tablespoons = 1 cup = 236 milliliters = .236 liters (¼ liter, approx.)

4 cups = 1 quart = .946 liters (1 liter, approx.)

1 milliliter = ⅕ teaspoon

1 liter = 1.057 quarts

4 liters = 1 gallon plus 1 cup

Oven Settings

American Oven Degrees Fahrenheit	Degrees Celsius
140°–250° Low or "Slow"	70°–121°
300°–400° Moderate	150°–205°
400° up High or "Hot"	205° up

Endnotes

Chapter 1

1. www.cia.gov/cia/publications/factbook/geos/us.html

Chapter 2

1. Ehrenreich, Barbara, and Arlie Russell Hochschild. *Global Woman: Nannies, Maids, and Sex Workers in the New Economy.* 1st ed. (New York: Metropolitan Books, 2003).
2. Barnlund, Dean C. *Public and Private Self in Japan and the United States: Communicative Styles of Two Cultures.* 1st ed. (Tokyo; Portland, OR: Simul Press, 1975; distributed by ISBS).
3. Hall, Edward T. *The Hidden Dimension,* 1st ed. (Garden City, NY: Doubleday, 1966).
4. Schor, Juliet. *The Overspent American: Why We Want What We Don't Need.* (New York: Harper Perennial, 1999).
5. De Graaf, John, David Wann, and Thomas H. Naylor. *Affluenza: The All Consuming Epidemic.* 1st ed. (San Francisco, CA: Berrett-Koehler Publishers, 2001).

Chapter 3

1. *Census of the United States. 2000. www.census.gov.*
2. Kochman, Thomas. *Black and White Styles in Conflict* (Chicago: University of Chicago Press, 1981).
3. *Census of the United States. 2000. www.census.gov.*
4. Butterfield, Fox. "Why Asians Are Going to the Head of the Class," *New York Times,* 3 August, 1986.
5. Fussell, Paul. *Class: A Guide through the American Status System.* 1st ed. (New York: Summit Books, 1983).

Chapter 5

1. Guinier, Lani. *The Tyranny of the Majority: Fundamental Fairness in Representative Democracy* (New York: Free Press, 1994).

Chapter 7

1. Associated Press. "Many Gay Couples Contemplating Marriage Already Are Experienced Parents," *Boston Globe*, 21 March, 2004.

Chapter 13

1 http://releases.usnewswire.com/GetRelease.asp?id=35468
2. www.mcspotlight.org.
3. Schlosser, Eric. *Fast Food Nation: The Dark Side of the All-American Meal* (Boston: Houghton Mifflin, 2001).

Chapter 17

1. Underhill, Paco. *Why We Buy: The Science of Shopping* (New York: Simon & Schuster, 1999).

Chapter 20

1. www.themediaproject.com
2. Simmons, Rachel. *Odd Girl Out: The Hidden Culture of Aggression in Girls.* 1st ed. (New York: Harcourt, 2002).

Chapter 21

1. Schor, Juliet. *The Overworked American: The Unexpected Decline of Leisure* (New York: Basic Books, 1991).

Chapter 22

1. Brooks, David. "The Agenda: People Like Us." *Atlantic Monthly*, September, 2003.
2. Knefelkamp, L. Lee. Introductory remarks at the Summer Institute in Intercultural Communication. Portland, OR, 1999.
3. Lakoff, George, on *NOW With Bill Moyers*, aired July 23, 2004, Public Broadcast Service. www.pbs.org/now/politics/lakoff.html
4. Longworth, Richard C. "Global Economy Creates Divide," Chicago Tribune, 13 July, 1999.
5. Wolff, Edward N. *Top Heavy: The Increasing Inequality of Wealth in America and What Can Be Done about It.* Updated and expanded ed. (New York: New Press, 2002; distributed by W.W. Norton, 2002).
6. Castells, Manuel. *End of Millennium.* 2nd ed. Information age; v. 3, ed. M. Castells 2000, Oxford; Malden, MA: Blackwell.

Internet Resources

United States Government Resources
U.S. Department of Agriculture (www.usda.gov)
Department of the Treasury (www.ustreas.gov)
Alcohol, Firearms and Tobacco Bureau (www.atf.gov)
Customs and Border Patrol (www.customs.gov)
Centers for Disease Control (www.cdc.gov)
National "Do Not Call" Registry (www.donotcall.gov)
National Parks Service (www.nps.gov)
National Forest Service (www.fs.fed.us)
Listing of Federal Holidays each year (www.opm.gov/fedhol)

Free E-mail Addresses
Yahoo! (www.yahoo.com) or Hotmail (http://www.hotmail.com)

Resources for Buying New and Used Cars
Cars.com (www.cars.com) and Edmunds (www.edmunds.com)

Education Resources
National Association for the Education of Young Children (www.naeyc.org)
Network of Child Care Resource and Referral (www.nccrra.org)
Child Care Aware (www.childcareaware.org)
Magnet Schools of America (www.magnet.edu)
Charter Schools (www.uscharterschools.org)
National Association of Independent Schools (www.nais.org)
Council for American Private Education (www.capenet.org)

Miscellaneous
The American Immigration Lawyers Association (www.aila.org)
Slow Food U.S.A. (www.slowfoodusa.org)

Index